AP EUROPEAN HISTORY PRACTICE EXAMS

SPARK NOTES

SPARK PUBLISHING

AP exams, explanations, and study cards written by Barbara Gordon and Christian Sawyer.

SparkChart written by Rachel Chrastil.

Spark Publishing
120 Fifth Avenue
New York, NY 10011
www.sparknotes.com

ISBN-13: 978-1-4114-0488-5
ISBN-10: 1-4114-0488-2

Please submit changes or report errors to www.sparknotes.com/errors

Printed and bound in China.

CONTENTS

Acknowledgments v

Introduction 1

Format of the Exam 1
Scoring 3
How to Prepare for the Exam 3
Strategies for Taking the Exam 3
Registering for the Exam 4

Practice Exam 1 5

Practice Exam 1: Answers & Explanations 29

Section I: Multiple-Choice Explanations 32
Section II: Free-Response Explanations 42

Practice Exam 2 47

Practice Exam 2: Answers & Explanations 69

Section I: Multiple-Choice Explanations 72
Section II: Free-Response Explanations 82

ACKNOWLEDGMENTS

SparkNotes would like to thank the following writers and contributors:

David Futransky
AP European History teacher, Evanston Township High School, Evanston, Illinois

Barbara Gordon
AP European History teacher, Assumption High School, Louisville, Kentucky

Christian Sawyer
AP European History teacher, Hillsboro Comprehensive High School,
Nashville, Tennessee

INTRODUCTION

If you're looking at this book, you're probably at least considering taking the Advanced Placement European History Exam. And there are many good reasons to do so: AP exams give you the opportunity to earn valuable course credit or advanced standing in college, as well as the opportunity to impress on college admissions officers that you are a serious and dedicated student. AP exams offer one of the few chances to *prove* to colleges that you are already capable of doing college-level work.

In fact, the AP exams have become so highly touted, surrounded with so many expectations about what they say about you and what they can do for you, that it's easy for you to become overwhelmed or intimidated. We're here to tell you that the exam is manageable. We're here to help.

Practice exams are one of the very best ways to study for the AP exams, because they take away some of the mystique and hype regarding the exams and allow you to get comfortable with what's actually on the exam. More important, they can help you understand what's *not* on the exam, so you don't waste your time striving for some elusive ideal of "college-level preparation." Practice exams will help you see the exam as it really is, so you know exactly what to expect.

Before launching right into the exams, we'll give you an overview of how the exam is structured and precisely what kinds of questions you'll see on it.

FORMAT OF THE EXAM

The Advanced Placement European History Exam is three hours and five minutes long and is divided into two parts:

- A 55-minute multiple-choice section, which counts for 50 percent of your score
- A 130-minute free-response section, which counts for 50 percent of your score

The Multiple-Choice Section

Format

Section I of the exam contains 80 multiple-choice questions, which you are given 55 minutes to complete. The questions test your knowledge of material usually covered in a college introductory European History course. Section I counts for 50 percent of your final score on the exam.

The multiple-choice questions are either questions or incomplete statements, followed by five suggested answers or completions. The exam-graders penalize you a quarter-point for each wrong answer, so you should only guess if you can eliminate two or more of the answer choices.

Topics of Questions

The multiple-choice questions fall into these basic topics:

- **From 1450 to the French Revolution and Napoleonic Era.** Approximately 50 percent of the questions (or 28 questions) cover the period from 1450 to the French Revolution and the Napoleonic Era.
- **From the French Revolution and Napoleonic Era to the Present.** Approximately 50 percent of the questions (or 28 questions) cover the period from the French Revolution and the Napoleonic Era to the Present.

Twenty to 30 percent of questions focus on cultural and intellectual themes, 30 to 40 percent on political and diplomatic themes, and 30 to 40 percent on social and economic themes. Many questions draw on knowledge of more than one chronological period or theme.

The Free-Response Section

Types of Questions

Section II of the exam, which counts for 50 percent of your final score, is a 130-minute free–response section broken into three parts:

- **Part A.** Part A consists of one document-based essay question. This question will usually focus on a specific period of time, and requires the student both to analyze and interpret the documents provided as well as apply his or her own knowledge of the time period to construct a coherent essay. The documents, including charts, graphs, cartoons, pictures, and articles, are unlikely to be familiar to the student. Part A begins with a required 15-minute reading period where students are encouraged to analyze the documents and plan their answer. Students then spend 45 minutes writing their response.
- **Part B.** Part B consists of two standard essay questions, of which the student will choose one to answer. Suggested time allotment for Part B is 5 minutes of planning and 30 minutes of writing.
- **Part C.** Part C consists of two standard essay questions, of which the student will choose one to answer. Suggested time allotment is 5 minutes of planning and 30 minutes of writing.

Generally, the four questions included in Parts B and C move chronologically in time; questions in Part B will address issues that occurred before those addressed in Part C. Neither the DBQ nor those questions in Parts B and C will exclusively address issues that occurred in the period 1980–present.

Scoring

In general, in order to receive a 3 you must answer 60 percent of the multiple-choice questions correctly. In the free-response section, the document-based essay question counts for 45 percent of your total Section II score, while each of the two standard essays counts for 27.5 percent of that score. Each essay is scored on a scale from 1–9:

8–9	High Score
6–7	Medium–High Score
5	Medium Score
3–4	Medium–Low Score
1–2	Low Score

Answers to the questions in this section will be judged on the strength of the thesis developed and quality of the argument rather than on factual information. For example, if you incorrectly identify the date of a battle in the Civil War in one of your essays, you will not be penalized.

SCORING

The AP exam is scored on a five-point scale.

5	Extremely well qualified
4	Well qualified
3	Qualified
2	Possibly qualified
1	No recommendation

HOW TO PREPARE FOR THE EXAM

The AP European History Exam not only tests your knowledge of facts but also your ability to analyze a set of facts and draw conclusions. These skills are tested in both sections of the exam and are by far the most important skills you need to get a high score. In other words, it's not enough that you know the dates of the major battles in World War II. You have to understand why the Battle of the Bulge was so crucial to the outcome of the war. Dates and presidents and other facts are important as well, but how you pull all that data together is what the AP graders are really looking for.

This is a skill that you can improve. The best way is to take a lot of practice exams. That's why we've included two full-length exams in this book. The more familiar you are with analysis questions, the better you'll get at them. While some multiple-choice questions will ask you to analyze a set of facts and draw conclusions, these skills will primarily be tested in the free-response section of the exam. The more practice you have writing timed essays, and developing quality thesis statements and supporting arguments, the better off you'll be on exam day.

STRATEGIES FOR TAKING THE EXAM

Multiple-Choice Questions

- Skim the questions first so you know what sorts of things you'll be reading for.
- Answer the questions you feel confident with first, skipping harder questions and saving them for last.
- Guess on questions when you can eliminate at least two wrong answers.
- Mark the questions you can't answer with a check—tackle all of these questions after you've gone through all of Section I.
- Cross off wrong answers on your exam itself.

Document-Based Questions

- Analyze the question prompt and figure out exactly what the question is asking.
- Once you have analyzed the prompt, then you can begin to look at the documents.
- Analyze the who/what/where/why/how of each document. These will serve as the basis of your essay.
- After you have scanned the documents, begin to create an outline. Sketch out a thesis statement and figure out the topic of each supporting paragraph.
- Now you can write your essay. Although you should quote sparingly, be sure to cite your sources.
- The highest scoring essays use the majority of the documents. Also, you should address the author's identity and his or her potential biases in order to receive a high-level score.

Free-Response Questions

- Underline key words in the question (often the prompt gives you important pieces of guidance on purpose or on kinds of things to look for).
- Read the prompt carefully, underlining and marking the key parts of the question.
- Brainstorm ideas for your thesis and the evidence you will use to support it.
- Outline your essay in the form of a thesis supported by reasons and evidence.
- Reread the prompt to make sure you havens't missed part of the question.
- Don't get hung up on perfect wording, spelling, etc.
- Don't get upset if you can't remember exact dates or names, as you won't be penalized for that in this section.
- If you run out of time, at least try and put down an outline of what you would like to have written for the essay. You won't get full credit, but you may be able to pick up a point or two.

REGISTERING FOR THE EXAM

Contact your school's AP coordinator or guidance counselor for help in registering for the exam. If you are home-schooled or your school does not administer the exam, contact AP Services for information about registering to take the exam at a school in your area that offers it.

AP Services
P.O. Box 6671
Princeton, NJ 08541-6671
(888) CALL-4AP; (609) 771-7300
TTY: (609) 882-4118
Email: apexams@ets.org
Website: www.collegeboard.com/ap/students/

PRACTICE EXAM 1

AP EUROPEAN HISTORY PRACTICE EXAM 1 ANSWER SHEET

1. Ⓐ Ⓑ Ⓒ Ⓓ Ⓔ	21. Ⓐ Ⓑ Ⓒ Ⓓ Ⓔ	41. Ⓐ Ⓑ Ⓒ Ⓓ Ⓔ	61. Ⓐ Ⓑ Ⓒ Ⓓ Ⓔ
2. Ⓐ Ⓑ Ⓒ Ⓓ Ⓔ	22. Ⓐ Ⓑ Ⓒ Ⓓ Ⓔ	42. Ⓐ Ⓑ Ⓒ Ⓓ Ⓔ	62. Ⓐ Ⓑ Ⓒ Ⓓ Ⓔ
3. Ⓐ Ⓑ Ⓒ Ⓓ Ⓔ	23. Ⓐ Ⓑ Ⓒ Ⓓ Ⓔ	43. Ⓐ Ⓑ Ⓒ Ⓓ Ⓔ	63. Ⓐ Ⓑ Ⓒ Ⓓ Ⓔ
4. Ⓐ Ⓑ Ⓒ Ⓓ Ⓔ	24. Ⓐ Ⓑ Ⓒ Ⓓ Ⓔ	44. Ⓐ Ⓑ Ⓒ Ⓓ Ⓔ	64. Ⓐ Ⓑ Ⓒ Ⓓ Ⓔ
5. Ⓐ Ⓑ Ⓒ Ⓓ Ⓔ	25. Ⓐ Ⓑ Ⓒ Ⓓ Ⓔ	45. Ⓐ Ⓑ Ⓒ Ⓓ Ⓔ	65. Ⓐ Ⓑ Ⓒ Ⓓ Ⓔ
6. Ⓐ Ⓑ Ⓒ Ⓓ Ⓔ	26. Ⓐ Ⓑ Ⓒ Ⓓ Ⓔ	46. Ⓐ Ⓑ Ⓒ Ⓓ Ⓔ	66. Ⓐ Ⓑ Ⓒ Ⓓ Ⓔ
7. Ⓐ Ⓑ Ⓒ Ⓓ Ⓔ	27. Ⓐ Ⓑ Ⓒ Ⓓ Ⓔ	47. Ⓐ Ⓑ Ⓒ Ⓓ Ⓔ	67. Ⓐ Ⓑ Ⓒ Ⓓ Ⓔ
8. Ⓐ Ⓑ Ⓒ Ⓓ Ⓔ	28. Ⓐ Ⓑ Ⓒ Ⓓ Ⓔ	48. Ⓐ Ⓑ Ⓒ Ⓓ Ⓔ	68. Ⓐ Ⓑ Ⓒ Ⓓ Ⓔ
9. Ⓐ Ⓑ Ⓒ Ⓓ Ⓔ	29. Ⓐ Ⓑ Ⓒ Ⓓ Ⓔ	49. Ⓐ Ⓑ Ⓒ Ⓓ Ⓔ	69. Ⓐ Ⓑ Ⓒ Ⓓ Ⓔ
10. Ⓐ Ⓑ Ⓒ Ⓓ Ⓔ	30. Ⓐ Ⓑ Ⓒ Ⓓ Ⓔ	50. Ⓐ Ⓑ Ⓒ Ⓓ Ⓔ	70. Ⓐ Ⓑ Ⓒ Ⓓ Ⓔ
11. Ⓐ Ⓑ Ⓒ Ⓓ Ⓔ	31. Ⓐ Ⓑ Ⓒ Ⓓ Ⓔ	51. Ⓐ Ⓑ Ⓒ Ⓓ Ⓔ	71. Ⓐ Ⓑ Ⓒ Ⓓ Ⓔ
12. Ⓐ Ⓑ Ⓒ Ⓓ Ⓔ	32. Ⓐ Ⓑ Ⓒ Ⓓ Ⓔ	52. Ⓐ Ⓑ Ⓒ Ⓓ Ⓔ	72. Ⓐ Ⓑ Ⓒ Ⓓ Ⓔ
13. Ⓐ Ⓑ Ⓒ Ⓓ Ⓔ	33. Ⓐ Ⓑ Ⓒ Ⓓ Ⓔ	53. Ⓐ Ⓑ Ⓒ Ⓓ Ⓔ	73. Ⓐ Ⓑ Ⓒ Ⓓ Ⓔ
14. Ⓐ Ⓑ Ⓒ Ⓓ Ⓔ	34. Ⓐ Ⓑ Ⓒ Ⓓ Ⓔ	54. Ⓐ Ⓑ Ⓒ Ⓓ Ⓔ	74. Ⓐ Ⓑ Ⓒ Ⓓ Ⓔ
15. Ⓐ Ⓑ Ⓒ Ⓓ Ⓔ	35. Ⓐ Ⓑ Ⓒ Ⓓ Ⓔ	55. Ⓐ Ⓑ Ⓒ Ⓓ Ⓔ	75. Ⓐ Ⓑ Ⓒ Ⓓ Ⓔ
16. Ⓐ Ⓑ Ⓒ Ⓓ Ⓔ	36. Ⓐ Ⓑ Ⓒ Ⓓ Ⓔ	56. Ⓐ Ⓑ Ⓒ Ⓓ Ⓔ	76. Ⓐ Ⓑ Ⓒ Ⓓ Ⓔ
17. Ⓐ Ⓑ Ⓒ Ⓓ Ⓔ	37. Ⓐ Ⓑ Ⓒ Ⓓ Ⓔ	57. Ⓐ Ⓑ Ⓒ Ⓓ Ⓔ	77. Ⓐ Ⓑ Ⓒ Ⓓ Ⓔ
18. Ⓐ Ⓑ Ⓒ Ⓓ Ⓔ	38. Ⓐ Ⓑ Ⓒ Ⓓ Ⓔ	58. Ⓐ Ⓑ Ⓒ Ⓓ Ⓔ	78. Ⓐ Ⓑ Ⓒ Ⓓ Ⓔ
19. Ⓐ Ⓑ Ⓒ Ⓓ Ⓔ	39. Ⓐ Ⓑ Ⓒ Ⓓ Ⓔ	59. Ⓐ Ⓑ Ⓒ Ⓓ Ⓔ	79. Ⓐ Ⓑ Ⓒ Ⓓ Ⓔ
20. Ⓐ Ⓑ Ⓒ Ⓓ Ⓔ	40. Ⓐ Ⓑ Ⓒ Ⓓ Ⓔ	60. Ⓐ Ⓑ Ⓒ Ⓓ Ⓔ	80. Ⓐ Ⓑ Ⓒ Ⓓ Ⓔ

AP EUROPEAN HISTORY

Three hours and 5 minutes are allotted for this examination: 55 minutes for Section I, which consists of multiple-choice questions, and 130 minutes for Section II, which consists of essay questions. 15 minutes of Section II are devoted to a mandatory reading period, primarily for the document-based essay question in Part A. Section I is printed in this examination booklet. Section II is printed in a separate booklet. In determining your grade, the two sections are given equal weight.

SECTION I

Time—55 minutes
Number of questions—80
Percent of total grade—50

Section I of this examination contains 80 multiple-choice questions. Therefore, please be careful to fill in only the ovals that are preceded by numbers 1 through 80 on your answer sheet.

General Instructions

DO NOT OPEN THIS BOOKLET UNTIL YOU ARE INSTRUCTED TO DO SO.

INDICATE YOUR ANSWERS TO QUESTIONS IN SECTION I ON THE SEPARATE ANSWER SHEET ENCLOSED. No credit will be given for anything written in this examination booklet, but you may use the booklet for notes or scratchwork. After you have decided which of the suggested answers is best, COMPLETELY fill in the corresponding oval on the answer sheet. Give only one answer to each question. If you change an answer, be sure that the previous mark is erased completely.

Example	Sample Answer
Chicago is a	Ⓐ Ⓑ Ⓒ ● Ⓔ

    (A) state
    (B) continent
    (C) country
    (D) city
    (E) village

Many candidates wonder whether or not to guess the answers to questions about which they are not certain. In this section of the examination, as a correction for haphazard guessing, one-fourth of the number of questions you answer incorrectly will be subtracted from the number of questions you answer correctly. It is improbable, therefore, that mere guessing will improve your score significantly; it may even lower your score, and it does take time. If, however, you are not sure of the best answer but have some knowledge of the question and are able to eliminate one or more of the answer choices as wrong, your chance of answering correctly is improved, and it may be to your advantage to answer such a question.

Use your time effectively, working as rapidly as you can without losing accuracy. Do not spend too much time on questions that are too difficult. Go on to other questions and come back to the difficult ones later if you have time. It is not expected that everyone will be able to answer the multiple-choice questions.

AP EUROPEAN HISTORY
SECTION I: MULTIPLE-CHOICE QUESTIONS
Time—55 minutes
80 Questions

<u>Directions:</u> Each of the questions or incomplete statements below is followed by five suggested answers or completions. Select the one that is best in each case and then fill in the corresponding oval on the answer sheet.

1. Which is true regarding French Calvinism in the latter half of the sixteenth century?

   (A) It was weakening as a liberal religious faction in the fringe areas of France.
   (B) A significant percentage of the French aristocracy aligned itself with the Huguenots not only for religious motivations but largely as a means of increasing the trend in political decentralization in France.
   (C) The king embraced Calvinism as a viable alternative to French Catholicism.
   (D) Calvinism became a radically emotional branch of Protestantism that advocated against child baptism.
   (E) Calvinism was especially attractive to the manual laborers in France seeking spiritual recognition.

2. Although he was initially popular, Napoleon III lost prestige because

   I.   he made an unpopular alliance with Georges Clemenceau, a radical
   II. France made a huge financial and military effort to give Prince Maximilian control of Mexico
   III. France joined the losing side of the Crimean War
   IV. France was soundly defeated by the Prussians

   (A) I and III
   (B) III and IV
   (C) II and IV
   (D) I, II, and III
   (E) I, II, III, and IV

3. The Treaty of Chaumont should be associated with the

   (A) Three Emperors' League
   (B) Quadruple Alliance
   (C) Continental system
   (D) Second Moroccan crisis
   (E) Entente Cordiale

4. Fifteenth-century Portuguese exploration was inspired most by which of the following motives?

   (A) A missionary fervor to diffuse Catholicism throughout the world
   (B) A desire to achieve commercial command of the gold and spice trade
   (C) A desire to investigate new lands
   (D) A competition with Islam
   (E) A need to bring home exotic goods for Portuguese nobility

5. The hacienda economy of Spanish colonies in the New World was characterized by

   (A) use of forced American and African laborers
   (B) the production of corn to feed the burgeoning European population
   (C) a plantation-structure agricultural model
   (D) a respect for indigenous Native American cultures by the conquering Spanish
   (E) both A and C

6. According to Castiglione in his *Book of the Courtier*, the "Renaissance man" should

   (A) be solely committed to the teachings of the Catholic orthodoxy
   (B) understand that biblical teachings are paramount to success in life
   (C) be adroitly critical of all social change
   (D) be of good birth and strong training in all aspects of social grace and liberal arts
   (E) not attempt studying useless languages such as Latin but rather focus on the vernacular

7. All of the following are reasons for the extraordinary growth of Italian city–states during the Renaissance EXCEPT

   (A) infighting that distracted papal control over the city–states
   (B) Italy's geographic position
   (C) political unity of the Italian city–states
   (D) the amassing of wealth in the Italian merchant class
   (E) a competitive spirit among the Italian regions

GO ON TO THE NEXT PAGE

8. Russia's Peter I (the Great) is most associated with

   (A) establishing increased monarchial control over the Russian church
   (B) attempting to reject all Western influence in Russia
   (C) moving the capital from Kiev to Uglich
   (D) relieving the economic burden of the peasants
   (E) de-centralizing the Russian government

9. Renaissance humanists embraced all of the following EXCEPT

   (A) a suspicion of pleasure grounded in materialism
   (B) a love for antiquity and its usefulness in seeking virtue
   (C) a devotion to civic responsibility
   (D) a commitment to liberal education for practical purposes
   (E) the dissemination of orthodoxy to bolster support for Christianity

10. Which of the following observation(s) is/are most accurate in depicting contrasts between medieval and Renaissance art?

   I. Renaissance art observed the natural world, while medieval art was prefigured to meet formulaic expectations.
   II. Renaissance art mirrored a sense of balance in the universe, while medieval art did not attempt for such rationality.
   III. Medieval art reflected the use of greater artistic shading, while Renaissance art avoided shading.
   IV. Renaissance art focused more on the individual in an autonomous plane, while medieval art saw the person as being more intrinsically linked to social institutions such as the Church.

   (A) I, II, and III
   (B) III and IV only
   (C) I, II, and IV
   (D) II and III only
   (E) I, II, III, and IV

11. All of the following Protestant leaders should be grouped together EXCEPT

   (A) Martin Luther
   (B) Henry VIII
   (C) John Calvin
   (D) John Knox
   (E) Ulrich Zwingli

12. Who, among the following leaders, is (are) most associated with being a *politique* leader?

   (A) Philip II of Spain
   (B) Oliver Cromwell in England
   (C) Mary I of England
   (D) Elizabeth I of England and Henry IV of France
   (E) Henry VIII of England

13. One of the longer-reaching effects of the plague on the urban economy of fourteenth-century Western Europe was that it

   (A) fueled a growth in apprenticeships and training of skilled artisans to meet the rising demand for luxury items
   (B) caused social panic in the countryside, resulting in a fear of the cities
   (C) caused an emigration from cities to the countryside, thereby restricting the supply of urban labor
   (D) weakened the voice of the guilds, thereby loosening the protection of local industries
   (E) caused a surplus of expensive goods that led to price deflation

14. Saint Bartholomew's Day in France, 1572, was significant in that it

   (A) internationalized the conflict between Catholics and Protestants
   (B) pushed France into a civil war
   (C) pacified the French Huguenots
   (D) pushed the Guises out of power in France
   (E) both A and B

15. "The true Church could do without such elaborate possessions and ornaments. Furthermore, the Church, in its ostentatious form, may not be necessary for salvation, since devout Christians could read the Bible when translated into the vernacular."

   The quote above would most likely be attributed to

   (A) Wycliff, Huss, or Luther
   (B) Johann Tetzel
   (C) St. Ignatius of Loyola or a Jesuit
   (D) Catherine de Medici
   (E) Holy Roman Emperor Charles V

16. The launching of the Spanish Armada in 1588 was motivated by

   (A) a desire to re-Catholicize England
   (B) sea-based disputes between England and Spain
   (C) Spain's wish to weaken English sea supremacy
   (D) Spanish nationalism
   (E) all of the above

GO ON TO THE NEXT PAGE

17. Which of the following accurately captures Martin Luther's attitude toward the German peasantry?

    (A) Luther called the peasants to overthrow the chains of their oppression and to reform the Church.
    (B) Luther denounced the peasants' calls for social revolution and instead embraced the German property-owning classes.
    (C) Luther largely ignored the existence of the peasants and focused only on Church reform.
    (D) Luther worked to bring the peasants into an agenda for social reform through careful political maneuvering.
    (E) Luther was generally critical of the treatment of the peasantry but did not make statements related to their situation.

18. The Pan-German League desired

    (A) more *lebensraum*
    (B) a strong alliance among all German-speaking nations
    (C) the unification of Germany
    (D) expansion into Africa
    (E) to gain a sphere of influence in China

19. Which of the following contributed to the maritime revolution of the sixteenth century?

    I. The development of the caravel
    II. The invention of the astrolabe
    III. Improved maps
    IV. The land-based trade route to China, which became very dangerous after the fall of the Mongols

    (A) I and III
    (B) II and III
    (C) I, II, and III
    (D) II, III, and IV
    (E) I, II, III, and IV

20. Where was the Protestant Reformation strongest?

    (A) Italy
    (B) France and Spain
    (C) Germany, Switzerland, and Netherlands
    (D) Romania and Russia
    (E) there was no geographic trend

21. Between the sixteenth and nineteenth centuries, Western European family life was largely characterized by all of the following EXCEPT

    (A) a later age for marrying than in previous centuries
    (B) familiarity with infant and child death
    (C) widespread remarriage by widows and widowers soon after their spouses' deaths
    (D) forced arranged marriages
    (E) the use of wet nurses by the upper nobility

22. The Council of Trent (1545–1562) served primarily to

    (A) reform the Catholic Church's teachings and beliefs
    (B) embrace groups like the Jansenists
    (C) reform internal church practices and organizational structure
    (D) counter the progress of the Protestant reformers
    (E) both C and D

23. Disregarding the political and personal reasons for his religious conversion, Henry VIII's religious beliefs most closely align with mainstream

    (A) Catholicism
    (B) Calvinism
    (C) Lutheranism
    (D) Eastern Orthodoxy
    (E) Judaism

24. The Reformation and Counter-Reformation influenced education in Western Europe by

    I. encouraging reform and realignment of curricula around humanist ideals
    II. reducing access to education for women
    III. increasing the number of Church-sponsored schools
    IV. improving literacy

    (A) I and IV
    (B) I, III, and IV
    (C) IV only
    (D) II and III
    (E) I, II, III, and IV

GO ON TO THE NEXT PAGE

25. Which of the following contributed to the spread of the Protestant faith in German-speaking areas?

    I.   Many German rulers wanted greater political independence from the Papacy.
    II. Tithing to Rome would cease.
    III. Many northerners opposed the use of church funds for art and building projects.
    IV. Theological disputes over the sale of indulgences

    (A) I and IV
    (B) II and III
    (C) I, II, and III
    (D) II, III, and IV
    (E) I, II, III, and IV

26. "The joining of religious confidence with self-disciplined activism produced an ethic that fueled the birth of capitalistic success."

    The quote above captures the essence of whose work?

    (A) John Calvin
    (B) Ulrich Zwingli
    (C) Max Weber
    (D) Charles V
    (E) Ignatius of Loyola

27. The year 1492 is significant in Spanish history because

    (A) Muslims who had held Granada were defeated and Spain was unified
    (B) Cordoba was captured by Ferdinand's forces
    (C) Columbus's voyage was sponsored by Ferdinand and Isabella
    (D) A and C
    (E) A, B, and C

28. All of the following took similar approaches in their treatment of people they encountered in the New World EXCEPT

    (A) Christopher Columbus
    (B) Ferdinand Magellan
    (C) Hernando Cortes
    (D) Bartolomé de las Casas
    (E) Francisco Pizarro

29. A political or economic event that directly followed the policies of mercantilism was

    (A) Philip II's control of lands in the Americas
    (B) Bismarck's emphasis on strong industry
    (C) the Netherlands' attempt to gain independence from Spain
    (D) Britain's industrial era
    (E) the Thirty Years' War

30. The seventeenth-century bourgeoisie, especially in France and Britain, were able to gain a degree of political importance by

    (A) petitions to the royal family
    (B) purchase of estates
    (C) marriage to an aristocrat
    (D) purchasing clerical titles
    (E) B and C

GO ON TO THE NEXT PAGE

AP EUROPEAN HISTORY MULTIPLE-CHOICE QUESTIONS

31. The following is an excerpt from "The Court of Louis XIV" by Duc de Saint-Simon, a longtime resident and courtier at Versailles:

"Glory was his (Louis XIV) passion, but he also liked order and regularity in all things; he was naturally prudent, moderate, and reserved; always a master of his tongue and emotions…His ministers, generals, mistresses, and courtiers soon found out his weak point, namely his love of hearing his own praises…The coarser and clumsier it was, the more he relished it…He loved splendor, magnificence and profusion in all things, and encouraged similar tastes in his court to spend money freely…By making expensive habits the fashion and for people in a certain position a necessity, he compelled his courtiers to live beyond their income…This was a plague which, once introduced, became a scourge to the whole country…This folly, sustained by pride and ostentation, has already produced widespread confusion; it threatens to end in nothing short of ruin and a general overthrow."

Which of the following statements can be inferred from the above passage?

I. Individual deficit spending was encouraged by Louis XIV.
II. Louis XIV was indifferent to clumsy efforts at flattering him.
III. St. Simon would not have been surprised at the financial crisis preceding the French Revolution.
IV. Louis XIV was personally thoughtful and rational.

(A) I and II
(B) I and III
(C) II and III
(D) I, III, and IV
(E) I, II, III, and IV

32. Who is the father of modern physics?

(A) Galileo
(B) Pascal
(C) Leibnitz
(D) Descartes
(E) Newton

33. Which of the following scientists is associated with heliocentrism, the theory that the earth revolved in a circular pattern around the sun?

(A) Galileo
(B) Copernicus
(C) Kepler
(D) Newton
(E) Bacon

34. In his *Second Treatise of Government*, John Locke established an argument for which of the following?

(A) Absolute monarchy
(B) Religious uniformity
(C) Democracy
(D) Limited authority
(E) Divine-right rule

35. Enlightenment philosophes agreed that

(A) human problems could best be solved through mathematics
(B) human suffering would end and progress would be promoted through the employment of reason and science
(C) rulers should be absolute
(D) the Catholic Church should be the supreme authority on difficult issues
(E) mercantilism was the preferred economic policy to promote human wealth and prosperity

36. Sixteenth- and seventeenth-century scientific and political ideas were accompanied by all of the following EXCEPT

(A) increasing conformity to tradition
(B) the movement of political theory away from a religious focus
(C) a fundamental challenge to medieval thought
(D) questioning of Church teachings
(E) new fears related to devil worship and superstition

37. The key component of the Schlieffen Plan was to

(A) defeat France quickly by invading from the north
(B) keep Russia neutral until the western offensive had begun
(C) maintain the neutrality of Belgium and the Netherlands
(D) have adequate forces to fight a two-front war
(E) gain naval support from the Ottoman Empire in order to threaten the Suez Canal

38. One legacy of the Fronde in seventeenth-century France was

(A) the establishment of constitutional monarchy
(B) Louis XIV's deep-seated mistrust of the nobility
(C) the creation of a capitalist economy
(D) parliamentary rule in France
(E) a resurgence of women's rights in France

GO ON TO THE NEXT PAGE

AP EUROPEAN HISTORY MULTIPLE-CHOICE QUESTIONS

39. Jingoism is associated with which of the following?

    (A) Spanish conquest of the New World
    (B) German excursions into southern Africa
    (C) Use of British force in the later 1800s
    (D) Unification of Germany
    (E) Anti-Chinese feelings in the West

40. Louis XIV's treatment of Jansenists

    (A) led to greater religious tolerance in France
    (B) increased religious disunity in France
    (C) increased his support among French Huguenots
    (D) aggravated the Jesuits
    (E) indicated a tone of *politique* style in his leadership

41. Which of the following statements is/are not true about the English Civil War?

    I.   The Cavaliers supported the rights of the peasants and middle class.
    II. The Cavaliers lost; the Roundheads won.
    III. Cromwell eventually took the title Lord Protector.
    IV. Charles I was executed at the end of the war.

    (A) I and II
    (B) II and III
    (C) I, II, and III
    (D) II, III, and IV
    (E) I, II, III, and IV

42. Which of the following factors most contributed to Poland's failure to maintain a competitive position in Europe during the seventeenth and eighteenth centuries?

    (A) The lack of a strong, central authority
    (B) The weakness of its nobility
    (C) Its reliance on mercantilism
    (D) A tradition of absolute monarchy
    (E) The absence of a national legislative body

43. During the reign of Queen Victoria of England, all of the following occurred EXCEPT

    (A) the Chartist movement
    (B) formation of the Fabian Society
    (C) formation of the Labour Party
    (D) Irish independence in the south of Ireland
    (E) adoption of the secret ballot

44. Peter the Great of Russia is associated with all of the following EXCEPT

    (A) weakening the control of the Russian nobility
    (B) building a new capital city for Russia
    (C) reorganizing internal organization of the government and administration
    (D) establishing a clear line of succession to his rule
    (E) attempting to incorporate western ideas into his eastern kingdom

GO ON TO THE NEXT PAGE

A FAUT ESPERER Q'EU JEU LA FINIRA BEN TOT.

L'tuteur en Campagne Ap. 1789.

45. Many late-eighteenth-century French political cartoons showed a thin, poorly clad person holding and supporting two other people, both of whom were well dressed, clean, and well fed. These cartoons addressed the issue of

   (A) the power of the clergy over the monarchy and bourgeoisie
   (B) the failure of French society to industrialize
   (C) Louis XVI's inability to work with his finance ministers
   (D) the three Estates, the third of which paid virtually all taxes
   (E) the failure of the Catholic Church to establish a working relationship with French Protestant minorities

GO ON TO THE NEXT PAGE

AP EUROPEAN HISTORY MULTIPLE-CHOICE QUESTIONS

46. In the crisis following the assassination of the Archduke Franz Ferdinand, Germany became involved when

    (A) William II offered to mediate between Serbia and Austria-Hungary
    (B) German ambassadors agreed to meet with Russia
    (C) the first of the other European nations began to mobilize
    (D) William II promised to support Austria
    (E) German forces invaded Serbia

47. Jacques Brissot's government failed in part because

    I.   the war with Austria and Prussia was not going well
    II. France continued to suffer from economic hardships
    III. radical politicians actively worked against Brissot's policies
    IV. the Gironde remained loyal to the Bourbon monarchy

    (A) I and II
    (B) II and III
    (C) I, II, and III
    (D) II, III, and IV
    (E) I, II, II, and IV

48. Machiavelli, in *The Prince*, said of governing that

    (A) ideally a ruler should be both feared and loved
    (B) a ruler's citizens need to be ruthlessly treated
    (C) a ruler may take any liberties with any citizen
    (D) rewards should rarely be given, so as not to raise unrealistic expectations
    (E) A and C

49. The main goal of the Congress of Vienna was to

    (A) dismantle the Napoleonic code in France
    (B) create a buffer zone between Austria and the Ottoman Empire
    (C) restore the legitimate pre-Napoleonic families to power and return France to its original territory
    (D) establish Finland as an independent nation
    (E) divide Prussia into three parts

50. Great Britain did not formally align with the Confederate States of America, in part because

    (A) Britain desired no competition in the African slave market
    (B) Britain's economic need for cotton was supplied by Egypt
    (C) the British aristocracy had stronger religious and social ties with the North
    (D) the British government did not wish to alarm the large Irish immigrant population in the North
    (E) the South followed a policy of isolationism

51. Adam Smith favored an economic policy of

    (A) encouraging royal monopolies
    (B) expanding the aristocracy's role in trade
    (C) laissez-faire
    (D) increasing tariffs to promote nationalist industry
    (E) expanding Britain's textile industry

52. Which of the following are NOT correctly paired?

    (A) James Watt—steam engine
    (B) Richard Arkwright—water frame
    (C) Josiah Wedgewood—pyrometer
    (D) Samuel Morse—telephone
    (E) Robert Fulton—steamship

53. While Austria, Prussia, and Russia strengthened in power in the last half of the seventeenth century, which three states weakened in power?

    I.   Ottoman Empire
    II. Sweden
    III. France
    IV. England
    V.   Poland

    (A) I, IV, and V
    (B) I, II, and IV
    (C) I, II, and V
    (D) III, IV, and V
    (E) II, III, and IV

GO ON TO THE NEXT PAGE

© Art Resource

54. In this painting, Delacroix's goal is to

   (A) promote equality for nineteenth-century women
   (B) demonize the Ottoman Turks
   (C) idealize the Greeks' efforts to gain independence
   (D) advocate European neutrality regarding the Greek War
   (E) suggest the futility of Greek efforts at independence

GO ON TO THE NEXT PAGE

AP EUROPEAN HISTORY MULTIPLE-CHOICE QUESTIONS

55. Charles X enraged the French when he

   (A) attempted to limit the number of eligible voters and dissolve the Chamber of Deputies
   (B) attempted to annex Belgium
   (C) made a peace treaty with the Ottoman Empire
   (D) unleashed his soldiers in a bloody raid to stem the liberal movement
   (E) opposed Greek independence

56. All of the following were directly involved in Italian unification EXCEPT

   (A) Camillo di Cavour
   (B) Guiseppe Mazzini
   (C) Guiseppe Garibaldi
   (D) Victor Emmanuel II
   (E) Charles Albert

57. Many causes and events fueled the revolutions of 1848. The most important among these issues was that

   (A) German nationalists sought to annex portions of France and Austria
   (B) food shortages and high prices for food were common
   (C) France continued threatening domination in Western Europe
   (D) the anarchist movement was widespread, especially in northwestern Europe
   (E) Britain expelled radical leaders from its borders

58. An accurate generalization about the Hundred Years' War was that it was

   (A) diffused by the onset of the Black Death
   (B) primarily religious in nature and focused on early Protestant-Catholic tensions
   (C) solely related to the English claim to the French throne
   (D) as much about national identity as it was about territory
   (E) slowed the transition in France from feudalism to a more centralized state

59. "One thinks himself the master of others, and still remains a greater slave than they. As long as a people is compelled to obey, and obeys, it does well; as soon as it can shake off the yoke and shakes it off, it does still better…"

   The statement above most closely reflects the beliefs of which era?

   (A) Enlightenment
   (B) Age of Exploration
   (C) Renaissance
   (D) Counter-Reformation
   (E) Modernism

GO ON TO THE NEXT PAGE

THE NEW YEAR'S GIFT.

Pam (to Sir Colin). "WELL—UPON MY WORD—EH!—I'M REALLY EXTREMELY OBLIGED TO YOU—BUT—EH!—HOW ABOUT KEEPING THE BRUTE?"

© Punch Cartoon Library

60. The cartoonist is implying which of the following?

   I.   India was fully subdued.
   II. Lord Palmerston did not want British control over India.
   III. The political situation in India was very tense.
   IV. British authority in India was not guaranteed.

   (A) I
   (B) III and IV
   (C) I, II, and III
   (D) II, III, and IV
   (E) I, II, III, and IV

GO ON TO THE NEXT PAGE

AP EUROPEAN HISTORY MULTIPLE-CHOICE QUESTIONS

61. Ideals of the Victorian age regarding domesticity and familial roles stressed that

    (A) women should strive to work outside the home while still being a wife and mother
    (B) a woman's primary goal in life should be being a good wife and mother
    (C) both men and women should be fully and equally involved in the care of home and family
    (D) children should be educated in the home
    (E) extended families were superior to the nuclear unit

62. Which of the following is a late eighteenth century artistic and intellectual movement that reacted against the rationalism of the Enlightenment and stressed emotion and a celebration of nature?

    (A) Impressionism
    (B) Realism
    (C) Surrealism
    (D) Romanticism
    (E) Baroque

63. All of the following should be associated with medicine and health in the nineteenth century EXCEPT

    (A) Robert Koch
    (B) Florence Nightingale
    (C) Joseph Lister
    (D) Michael Faraday
    (E) Louis Pasteur

64. Pugachev's Rebellion in Russia (1773–75) reflected the growing discontent between Catherine the Great and

    (A) the Russian nobility
    (B) the Orthodox Church
    (C) the Russian peasantry
    (D) political prisoners
    (E) the philosophes

65. The sixteenth and seventeenth centuries saw a search for methods to improve farming production largely because of

    (A) the pressures of a growing European population
    (B) the failure of feudal farming methods
    (C) shortages of available farmland
    (D) the stability of low grain prices allowing innovation
    (E) both A and C

66. The Enclosure Movement in eighteenth-century England most significantly

    (A) provided the labor supply to rural regions for farming
    (B) introduced a capitalistic spirit into rural farming practices
    (C) opened private lands to public farming
    (D) gave peasants the right to farm more land
    (E) reduced the hostility between landlords and peasant farmers

GO ON TO THE NEXT PAGE

67. By 1800, approximately what percentage of inhabitants in France and Great Britain lived in cities?

    (A) 90
    (B) 75
    (C) 50
    (D) 20
    (E) 5

68. The mercantilist economic model was used in attempting to achieve all of the following goals EXCEPT

    (A) creating a national monopoly
    (B) securing a network of raw materials to feed industrial growth
    (C) controlling the world's limited resources
    (D) directing the national economy away from gold and silver bullion
    (E) limiting government regulation of trade

69. Utilitarianism of the nineteenth century advocated the idea that

    (A) all laws were equally good
    (B) laws and actions should be judged by their impact on the greatest number of people
    (C) all laws and governments should be abolished
    (D) religion was irrelevant
    (E) personal faith, not institutional religion, should be encouraged

70. The Fashoda incident and the Moroccan crisis indicated that

    (A) Americans and Europeans would not cooperate financially
    (B) Britain would not be able to hold a large empire
    (C) European powers might go to war over imperial holdings
    (D) European powers were intent on destroying the Ottoman Empire
    (E) China would be the next desired area for imperial conquest

71. Britain gained its initial economic and political role in India by

    (A) the actions and policies of the East India Company
    (B) treaties with the Mughal princes
    (C) the defeat of the Sepoys
    (D) the Seven Years' War
    (E) the defeat of Tipu Sultan's forces in the south

GO ON TO THE NEXT PAGE

AP EUROPEAN HISTORY MULTIPLE-CHOICE QUESTIONS

Employment in the Lancashire Cotton Industry, 1801–61

Date	Number of Workers in Industry	% of Working Population
1801	242,000	35.9
1811	306,000	36.9
1821	369,000	35.0
1831	427,000	31.9
1841	374,000	22.4
1851	379,000	18.6
1861	446,000	18.3

72. The information in the table above indicates that

(A) Britain's industrial production increased at a greater rate than any other European nation except Germany's
(B) women were a major component of textile production in England
(C) the growing industrial employment sector was expanding beyond Lancashire in the mid- to late-nineteenth century
(D) militarism caused manufacturing to increase in Western Europe
(E) 1801–61 was a time of economic stagflation in England

73. All of the following regarding Britain's involvement in southern Africa are true EXCEPT

(A) the discovery of gold and diamonds in the Transvaal increased British settlement there
(B) the British feared Germany would support the Boers
(C) the Boers bitterly resented British incursions into their territory
(D) the British placed Boer civilians in concentration camps to deter guerrilla efforts
(E) the Boers enlisted military assistance from the Zulus

74. The goal of the Decembrist revolt was to

(A) extend Russian control after its success in the Crimean War
(B) overthrow the Okhrana
(C) enact reforms in Russian government
(D) institute a policy of Pan-Slavism
(E) adopt a Western-style republican form of government and abolish the monarchy

75. Much of the Baroque art in southern Europe focused on religious themes largely because

(A) the Catholic Church was failing in Italy
(B) the Catholic Church was engaged in the Counter-Reformation
(C) the Hapsburgs were defeated in Spain
(D) Louis XIV became Protestant
(E) it was funded by the Protestant aristocracy

GO ON TO THE NEXT PAGE

76. Which of the following essential questions is most associated with the English Civil War?

    (A) Would England allow slavery in its colonial policies?
    (B) Would England enter into the War of Devolution?
    (C) Would England be a mercantile or capitalistic economy?
    (D) Would England be ruled by a parliamentary government or an absolute monarchy?
    (E) Would Anglicanism be allowed in England?

77. Bismarck's alliance system failed when

    (A) Nicholas II came to the Russian throne
    (B) Kaiser Wilhelm II abandoned the Russian portion of the second Three Emperors' League
    (C) Austria withdrew from the Dual Alliance
    (D) England sought to ally with the newly created Italian state
    (E) Germany attempted to extend its influence in the Balkans

78. Otto von Bismarck pursued which of the following policies?

    I.   Isolation of France
    II. Major expansion of the German navy
    III. Increased cooperation with Russia and Austria
    IV. Providing social welfare to working-class Germans

    (A) III
    (B) I and IV
    (C) I, II, and III
    (D) I, III, and IV
    (E) I, II, III, and IV

79. In World War I, the Allies sought to undermine the Ottoman Empire by

    (A) blockading the Dardanelles
    (B) aiding the Armenians against the Turks
    (C) encouraging divisions between the social classes
    (D) promising independence to areas such as Persia and Egypt if they revolted
    (E) employing anti-Turkish propaganda

80. Which of the following describes the significance of Lech Walesa's rise to power in Poland in 1989?

    (A) His political success indicated the end of the Cold War.
    (B) Through his leadership, Solidarity fought for workers' rights in a country focused on the ruling elite.
    (C) His work caused the fall of the Soviet Empire in Eastern Europe.
    (D) His election marked the first non-Communist government in the Soviet bloc.
    (E) He called for a return to socialized health care and worker's compensation.

IF YOU FINISH BEFORE YOUR TIME IS CALLED,
YOU MAY CHECK YOUR WORK ON THIS SECTION.
DO NOT GO ON TO SECTION II UNTIL YOU ARE TOLD TO DO SO.

END OF SECTION I

AP EUROPEAN HISTORY
SECTION II
Part A

(Suggested planning and writing time—45 minutes)
Percent of Section II score—45

<u>Directions:</u> The following question is based on the accompanying Documents 1–9.

This question is designed to test your ability to work with historical documents. As you analyze the documents, <u>take into account both the sources of the documents and the authors' points of view</u>. Write an essay on the following topic that integrates your analysis of the documents. **Do not simply summarize the documents individually.** You may refer to relevant historical facts and developments not mentioned in the documents.

1. Evaluate the changing role of French women as a result of the 1789 revolution.

    Historical Background: In 1789 Louis XVI called for a meeting of the representative body called the Estates General in order to solve France's severe economic crisis. What ensued would be an escalating social and political revolution that ended the monarchy in France and established a republic. The liberal forces would eventually gain the upper hand, affecting the entire European continent. Most historians consider the end of the revolution to have occurred when Napoleon overthrew the Directory in 1799.

Document 1

An engraving about French hairstyles, circa 1788

GO ON TO THE NEXT PAGE

Document 2

We (the petitioners) prefer, Sire, to place our cause at your feet; not wishing to obtain anything except from your heart, it is to it that we address our complaints and confide our miseries. The women of the Third Estate are almost all born without wealth; their education is very neglected or very defective...They are taught to work; having reached the age of fifteen or sixteen, they can earn five or six sous a day. If nature has refused them beauty they get married, without a dowry, to unfortunate artisans; lead aimless, difficult lives stuck in the provinces; and give birth to children they are incapable of raising. If, on the contrary, they are born pretty, without breeding, without principles, with no idea of morals, they become prey of the first seducer, commit a first sin, come to Paris to bury their shame, end by losing it all together, and die victims of dissolute ways...We ask to be enlightened, to have work, not in order to usurp men's authority, but in order to be better esteemed by them, so that we might have the means of living safe from misfortune...

—*Petition of Women of the Third Estate to the King*, 1789

Document 3

To Versailles, To Versailles

Women of Paris march to Versailles; October, 1789

© Getty Resources

GO ON TO THE NEXT PAGE

AP EUROPEAN HISTORY FREE-RESPONSE QUESTIONS

Document 4

…have they not all violated the principle of equality of rights by quietly depriving half of mankind of the right to participate in the formation of the laws, by excluding women from the rights of citizenship? Is there a stronger proof of the power of habit even among enlightened men than seeing the principle of equality of rights invoked in favor of three or four hundred men deprived of their rights by an absurd prejudice and at the same time forgetting those rights when it comes to twelve million women?… It would be difficult to prove that women are incapable of exercising the rights of citizenship…Either no individual in mankind has true rights or all have the same ones…Why should beings exposed to pregnancies and to passing indispositions not be able to exercise rights that no one ever imagined taking away from people who have gout every winter or who easily catch colds?… This observation (that women obey their feelings rather than their consciences) is truer but it proves nothing.

—A liberal Frenchman and member of the Academy of Science, (1743–1794)

Document 5

…All citizens, without distinction of birth, are eligible to any office or dignity, whether ecclesiastical, civil or military…

—Decree from the National Assembly, 1789

Document 6

Patriotic women come before you to claim the right which any individual has the right to defend his life and liberty…We are *citoyennes* (female citizens), and we cannot be indifferent to the fate of the fatherland…we need arms, and we come to ask your permission to procure them. May our weakness be no obstacle; courage and intrepidity will supplant it, and the love of the fatherland and our hatred of tyrants will allow us to brave all dangers…

—Pauline Leon, "Petition to the National Assembly on Women's Rights to Bear Arms"

Document 7

Article 6:
   The laws must be the expression of the general will; all female and male citizens must contribute either personally or through their representatives to its formation; it must be the same for all: male and female citizens, being equal in the eyes of the law, must be equally admitted to all honors, positions, and public employment according to their capacity and without other distinctions besides those of their virtues and talents.

—Olympe de Gouges, 1791

GO ON TO THE NEXT PAGE

Document 8

The National Assembly, considering the importance of enabling Frenchmen to enjoy the privilege of divorce, a consequence of individual liberty, which would be doomed by indissoluble engagements; considering already that a number of married couples have not waited, in order to enjoy the advantages of the constitutional provision according to which marriage is only a civil contract, until the law had regulated the manner and consequences of divorce, decrees as follows…Divorce shall take place by mutual consent by husband and wife.

—Divorce legislation from the National Assembly, 1792

Document 9

Equality holding a copy of the Declaration of the Rights of Man and Citizen

© Corbis

END OF PART A

GO ON TO THE NEXT PAGE ▶

AP EUROPEAN HISTORY
SECTION II
Parts B & C

(Suggested planning and writing time—70 minutes)
Percent of Section II score—55

<u>Directions:</u> You are to answer the following questions. You should spend 5 minutes organizing or outlining each essay. Write an essay that:

- has a relevant thesis and supports that thesis with appropriate historical evidence.
- addresses all parts of the question.
- uses historical context to show change over time and/or continuities.

1. Evaluate the following statement: "Martin Luther was the father of Protestantism."

2. Was Napoleon a revolutionary or reactionary, a liberal or a conservative? Evaluate the success and failures of his rule as you discuss their long-term impact on France and Europe. Include in your response social, economic, political, and legal factors.

END OF EXAMINATION

PRACTICE EXAM 1: ANSWERS & EXPLANATIONS

Answer Key for Practice Exam 1

Number	Answer	Right	Wrong	Number	Answer	Right	Wrong	Number	Answer	Right	Wrong
1	B	___	___	28	D	___	___	55	A	___	___
2	C	___	___	29	A	___	___	56	E	___	___
3	B	___	___	30	E	___	___	57	B	___	___
4	B	___	___	31	D	___	___	58	D	___	___
5	E	___	___	32	E	___	___	59	A	___	___
6	D	___	___	33	B	___	___	60	B	___	___
7	C	___	___	34	D	___	___	61	B	___	___
8	A	___	___	35	B	___	___	62	B	___	___
9	E	___	___	36	A	___	___	63	D	___	___
10	C	___	___	37	A	___	___	64	C	___	___
11	B	___	___	38	B	___	___	65	E	___	___
12	D	___	___	39	A	___	___	66	B	___	___
13	A	___	___	40	B	___	___	67	C	___	___
14	E	___	___	41	D	___	___	68	E	___	___
15	A	___	___	42	A	___	___	69	B	___	___
16	E	___	___	43	D	___	___	70	C	___	___
17	B	___	___	44	D	___	___	71	A	___	___
18	A	___	___	45	D	___	___	72	C	___	___
19	E	___	___	46	D	___	___	73	E	___	___
20	C	___	___	47	C	___	___	74	C	___	___
21	D	___	___	48	A	___	___	75	B	___	___
22	E	___	___	49	C	___	___	76	D	___	___
23	A	___	___	50	B	___	___	77	B	___	___
24	B	___	___	51	C	___	___	78	D	___	___
25	E	___	___	52	D	___	___	79	D	___	___
26	C	___	___	53	C	___	___	80	D	___	___
27	D	___	___	54	C	___	___				

HOW TO CALCULATE YOUR SCORE

Section I: Multiple Choice

[_____ – ($\frac{1}{4}$ × _____)] × 1.125 = _____

Number
Correct
(out of 80)

Number Wrong

Weighted
Section I Score
(Do not round.)

Section II: Free Response

Document-Based Essay _____ × 4.500 = _____

(out of 9)

Thematic Essay 1 _____ × 2.750 = _____

(out of 9)

Thematic Essay 2 _____ × 2.750 = _____

(out of 9)

Sum = _____

Weighted
Section II Score
(Do not round.)

Composite Score

_____ + _____ = _____

Weighted Section I
Score

Weighted Section II
Score

Composite Score
(Round to the nearest
whole number.)

Composite Score*	AP Grade	Interpretation
122–180	5	extremely well qualified
99–121	4	well qualified
66–98	3	qualified
45–65	2	possibly qualified
0–44	1	no recommendation

*Each year the Development Committee determines the formulas used to calculate the raw composite scores. The Chief Faculty Consultant determines how the composite scores fit into the 5-point AP scale.

1.   **B**

The rise of Calvinism was closely related to the growing dissatisfaction among the French aristocrats pushing for devolution from the controls of the weakened, Catholic French monarch and the Guises.

2.   **C**

Georges Clemenceau was a contemporary of Napoleon III, but the two were not allied. France was on the winning side of the Crimean War (though this was of little benefit).

3.   **B**

The Treaty of Chaumont was signed in 1814 and created the alliance of Prussia, Austria, Russia, and Britain. The Continental system, Napoleon's attempt to blockade Britain, occurred in 1806. The Second Moroccan crisis (1911) involved the German and French rivalry over Morocco. The Three Emperor's League (c. 1872) involved Germany, Russia, and Austria-Hungary. The Entente Cordiale was between France and England.

4.   **B**

While **A**, **C**, **D**, and **E** were certainly factors rationalizing Portuguese exploration, Portuguese explorers were ultimately directed toward dominating the Indian Ocean-based gold and spice trade to feed the insatiable European hunger for such goods and build personal and imperial wealth around such endeavors.

5.   **E**

The hacienda, or plantation, economy of the Spanish colonies was built upon the backs of the Native Americans, who were enslaved into this economic pattern to feed the extractive industries mining "New Spain" of its gold and silver ores. Choice **B** is incorrect, as the Spanish colonies were designed primarily to build gold and silver capital for the Empire. This was accomplished with little to no consideration of the natives of the land, thus making **D** incorrect.

6.   **D**

Castiglione, the archetype of liberal humanism, wrote that the ideal man should be well versed in all aspects of life, including literature, history, and even dance and song.

7.   **C**

The disunity among the Italian city–states only strengthened the opportunity for the individual regions to grow within themselves and compete for economic and social supremacy, generating a sense of competitive spirit that drove the innovation and creation typical of the Renaissance "rebirth."

8.   **A**

Peter the Great was known as a ruthless reformer who tried to westernize Russian culture. One of his most prominent advancements was establishing increased monarchial control over the Russian church.

9.   **E**

Renaissance humanists did not support the spread of orthodox Church beliefs for such ends, but saw a return to classical ideas and beliefs for the purpose of scholasticism and education.

10.   **C**

Renaissance artists employed the innovative technique of chiaroscuro, the use of shading to create a more natural representation of the subject. While medieval art focused on the supernatural and on religious themes, Renaissance art focused on the individual as its subject matter.

11.   **B**

Henry VIII's break from the Catholic Church occurred for purely political reasons; he wanted an immediate divorce from Catherine of Aragon. The other Protestants broke because of theological disputes with the Papacy.

12.   **D**

Elizabeth I and Henry IV exemplified *politique* style, subordinating religious conviction to political unity and moderation in their respective nations. The other leaders were unwilling to compromise their religious convictions, which were at the helm of their national agendas.

13.   **A**

The plague led to a growth in demand for luxurious goods in the second half of the fourteenth century, as people insisted on having luxury amidst such despair. The initial onslaught of the plague reduced the supply of skilled urban artisans, thereby reducing the ability of the market to meet the demand for such goods. This, then, lured the rural workers to the cities, as prices for such goods rose along with the pay for producing such goods, making **E** incorrect. Furthermore, with the deaths within the noble class, peasants were able to escape from their lords more easily to move into the cities, making **C** incorrect. **B** is incorrect because of the question's focus on long-reaching economic effects, and while panic did initially cause fear of the cities, that subsided in a general way.

14.   **E**

Saint Bartholomew's Day, 1572, saw a massacre of an estimated 19,000 Huguenots at the hands of French Catholics. This pushed French Calvinists to radicalize their call for religious freedoms and alarmed Protestants outside of France that this conflict was a struggle for survival.

15.   **A**

Oxford Professor John Wycliff expressed in 1380 much of the sentiments of the Lollards, who criticized the trappings of the Catholic Church's wealth when comparing it to the suffering of the poor in England. His ideas inspired John Huss and the Hussites, who eventually influenced Luther and the resulting Reformation.

16.   **E**

The Armada was not just an attempt to defeat English naval supremacy, but it was also an attempt by Philip II to overthrow Elizabeth and install a Catholic monarch in England.

17.   **B**

While Luther embraced the simple life of hard work lived by the peasantry, he condemned peasant uprisings and even urged German princes to crush their revolts without compassion and mercy. Luther made such a move to gain support among the nobility.

18.   **A**

The Pan-German League was created in 1891. Germany had already unified in 1871, making **C** incorrect. The Pan-German League, along with other organizations, argued that Germany was entitled to more space for its people (*lebensraum* meaning "living space"). **D** and **E** are too narrow in focus.

19.   **E**

All were contributing factors. The caravel, although smaller than traditional ships, was a superior vessel for long-distance travel, and the astrolabe allowed sailors to better determine their positions at sea. More accurate maps, from both Arab and European sources, were available, also aiding the development of maritime trade. By 1368, the Ming Dynasty had wrested China away from the Mongols, whose extensive naval trading system was abandoned in favor of a more intranational, isolationist economic plan. This allowed Western powers to develop their maritime interests relatively unchallenged.

20.   **C**

The Reformation diffused in a southwesterly direction from Germany, Switzerland, and the Netherlands.

21.   **D**

While parents played a role in selecting their children's spouses, forced arranged marriages did not widely occur, as emotional commitment was considered an integral component in a successful marriage.

22.   **E**

The Council of Trent was called to counteract the success of the Protestant Reformation by reforming the internal organizational structure of the Church, such as making bishops more visible in towns and requiring seminaries for educational purposes in every diocese. However, no doctrinal concessions were made at Trent, thereby reasserting the Church's confidence in its beliefs and its refusal to meet Protestant theological demands, making **A** and **B** wrong (the Jansenists supported alternative Catholic doctrine).

23.   **A**

While he redirected the power over the English Church from the pope to the king, Henry VIII asserted his and his state's commitment to Catholicism in acts such as the Six Articles of 1539, which reaffirmed traditional Catholic teachings and prohibited clerical marriage.

24.   **B**

An important cultural achievement of the Reformation was its emphasis on educational reform to include more humanist ideals in schools and improve universal literacy. The Catholic Church also increased its efforts to broaden its influence through education, and the Protestant movement advocated the education of women for religious purposes, making Number II incorrect.

25. E

Separation from the powerful Roman Catholic Church allowed for greater social, political, and economic independence for northern European countries such as Germany (reflected in Numbers I, II, and III). The Protestant movement began in Germany, where Martin Luther first published his *95 Theses* by nailing them to the door of his Wittenberg church. Luther's tract challenged the Church on several theological issues, including the selling of indulgences (Number IV).

26. C

It captures the primary idea in Weber's *The Protestant Ethic and Spirit of Capitalism* (1904), in which Weber contends that there is a strong relationship between Calvinism, other derivatives of Protestant Puritanism, and the growth of capitalism as a defining trait in modern society.

27. D

Cordoba was defeated and captured in 1236 by forces from Portugal and Castile. Granada's fall and Columbus's voyage occurred in 1492.

28. D

Although de las Casas was Spanish, he protested and fought for decent treatment of Native Americans. The others were explorers whose main concern was gaining land and gold.

29. A

Philip II's reign saw massive quantities of gold and silver (a goal of mercantilists) imported into Spain. Germany and Britain's industrial eras were capitalist, and the Netherlands' primary opposition to Spain was over religious differences.

30. E

Many of the bourgeoisie became extremely wealthy and could purchase large estates, which elevated them from merely being tradesmen. Their wealth also afforded them the possibility of offering large dowries, which appealed to many aristocrats, some of whom had declining fortunes. Petitions for rights by class were generally not undertaken in the 1600s in France, making **A** incorrect. Britain was largely Protestant in the seventeenth century, and in France high clerical seats were generally controlled by the nobility, making **D** incorrect.

31. D

Louis XIV did enjoy all attempts at flattery, including clumsy ones, which makes statement II incorrect. The rest of the statements are correct.

32. E

Newton initiated a new order of thought that embraced the idea that Earth and its parts conformed to an identifiable set of laws and patterns, a foundational concept for modern physics.

33. B

Copernicus published *On the Revolutions of the Heavenly Spheres*, wherein he asserted that the earth was not the center of the universe, but that it revolved around a larger star, the sun.

34. **D**

Locke's essential argument embraced a contractually limited sovereign restricted by natural law from gaining absolute power. Locke's ideas predicated the growth of liberalism in Britain.

35. **B**

Enlightenment thinkers were unified in their worship of human reason and measured observation in the form of science as the means to reaching a more perfect society. While the philosophes embraced mathematics because of its ordered, logical nature, they would not have all agreed that it was the means to reach such ends, making choice **A** incorrect.

36. **A**

The Scientific Revolution and Enlightenment were related to all options except for an increasing conformity to traditional thought, as this era embodied a growing spirit of questioning accepted authority and seeking knowledge in religious, scientific, social, and political realms.

37. **A**

The Schlieffen Plan, which was put into effect in 1914, was intended to prevent Germany from fighting a two-front war by defeating France quickly. To this end, Germany would invade northern France by going through Belgium and the Netherlands. The plan did not involve the Ottoman Empire, although Germany would ally with them in World War I.

38. **B**

The seventeenth-century chaos caused many to fear anarchy more than absolute rule, thereby paving the way for the archetype of divine-right rule, Louis XIV, who ruled France according to his declaration of "I am the State." Louis deeply distrusted the nobility after its attempt to overthrow him as a child in the Fronde, so he committed himself to suppressing them and relegating them to the most powerless position possible, in part through his creation of Versailles.

39. **A**

Jingoism, from a ditty using the phrase "but by Jingo, if we do (fight)" refers to Britain's increasing use of its navy and military in the late nineteenth century. This was done to promote its political and economic agendas.

40. **B**

Louis XIV supported the papal prohibition of Jansenism, which was an anti-Jesuit Catholic alternative. Louis XIV also supported the closing of Jansenist communities, causing them to go underground. His suppression of Jansenism fractured religious unity, thereby eliminating the image of religious peace in France.

41. **D**

The Cavaliers were the English nobles who wanted to maintain their elite status, thereby making Number I incorrect. The other statements are all true events dealing with the English Civil War.

42. **A**

Poland's monarchy was elective and simply a puppet of the controlling nobility, which exerted such power that it destroyed the possibility of national policy and unification, rendering Poland virtually anonymous in a political sense by the late 1750s. It was also partitioned by Russia, especially under Catherine the Great, and was surrounded by controlling neighbors.

43. **D**

Southern Ireland did not become independent until 1922; Victoria ruled from 1837 to 1901. The Chartist movement began in 1838, and the Fabians formed in 1858. The Labour Party was established in 1930.

44. **D**

Peter failed to provide a successor, as he had imprisoned his son, who died while in prison. Thus, upon Peter's death, chaos ensued as nobles fought for his title.

45. **D**

The old man in the cartoon represents the Third Estate (commoners), whose taxes financially supported the First and Second Estate (clergy and nobility), depicted here as riding on the old man's back. The clergy, while powerful, did not dominate the eighteenth-century French monarchy, and while Louis XVI did have problems in keeping a finance minister, the cartoon does not reflect this. It is also true that while the Catholic Church was disinterested in cordial relations with Protestant minorities and that France was slow to industrialize, these, also, are not reflected in the cartoon.

46. **D**

William II was initially enthusiastic about the war and encouraged Austria to be strong in its demands against Serbia, making **D** correct and **A** incorrect. Germany was one of the first European countries to get involved in World War I, making **C** incorrect. Germany did not initiate its involvement by invading Serbia, as suggested by **E**, but by declaring war on Serbia's ally, Russia (therefore making **B** false, as well.)

47. **C**

The Gironde, while reluctant to issue Louis XIV's death sentence, did not support or defend the Bourbons, thereby making Number IV incorrect. The remaining choices are all true statements: France suffered early losses to the Austrian and Prussian forces due to poor equipment and leadership. France's economic situation remained critical and the Jacobian faction turned increasingly hostile to the more moderate Gironde leaders.

48. **A**

Machiavelli did acknowledge that being both loved and feared was difficult but useful. However, he also advised that property and women should be treated as precious and that a wise ruler would provide rewards to worthy citizens on a regular basis.

49. **C**

The Congress of Vienna, which was very conservative in outlook, would have opposed the more liberal portions of the Napoleonic Code; however, the Congress was not concerned with France's internal laws. No buffer region was established between Austria and the Ottoman Empire. Russia had control of Finland, not France, and Prussia was divided into two parts, not three.

50.   **B**

England abolished slavery completely in 1834; by the time of the American Civil War, the British had no interests in the African slave market. The British generally had more in common with the Southern gentry, and the British government was not concerned with the Irish living in America. The South was not isolationist, but rather actively sought British support.

51.   **C**

Adam Smith espoused the laissez-faire doctrine, which favored no government interference with business on any level. Thus, **A** and **D** are incorrect. **B** and **E** are too narrow in focus to adequately convey Smith's economic philosophy.

52.   **D**

Samuel Morse invented the telegraph.

53.   **C**

After the Peace of Westphalia, the Austrian Hapsburgs actively sought to strengthen their position outside of Germany, while Prussia tried to protect its interests in Germany, and Russia drastically improved its military and naval capacities under the Romanovs—all of which came largely at the expense of Sweden, Poland, and the ailing Ottoman Empire.

54.   **C**

Delacroix painted *Greece Expiring on the Ruins of Missolonghi* (1826) in order to commemorate the Greek war of independence. The painting celebrates the heroism of the Greeks, thereby making **C** correct and **E** incorrect. The woman represents the suffering nation of Greece itself: the painting is not intended to promote equality for real women, as suggested by **A**. **B** is too strong a statement—there is nothing in the painting that specifically suggests that the Turks were excessively brutal in their actions against the Greeks. Many Romantics, such as Delacroix, advocated European involvement in the war, thereby making **D** incorrect.

55.   **A**

France supported Greek independence and was not a supporter of the Ottomans. The Congress of Vienna gave Belgium to the Netherlands. While Charles X was very conservative and deeply opposed to liberal views, he did not send troops to suppress the liberals but fled instead.

56.   **E**

Albert was a precursor in the process but had died before the actual unification efforts got underway, while the others were directly involved.

57.   **B**

Poor harvests, grain and potato diseases, and expanding populations combined to produce serious food shortages in many parts of Europe. German-speaking states and France were focused on internal issues (making **A** and **C** incorrect), and Britain allowed even radicals like Marx to remain (making **E** incorrect). The anarchist movement was more widespread in Eastern Europe (making **D** incorrect).

58. D

The Hundred Years' War pertained to English King Edward III's claim to Philip VI of Valois's French throne as well as to the territorial competition between the two countries over land such as Flanders, a French-owned land highly influenced by the English wool supply. **A** is incorrect in that the Bubonic Plague affected the countries involved but did not lead to a cessation of warfare. **B** is incorrect because both countries were Catholic. **E** is incorrect because the war had the opposite effect, as it ravaged much of the countryside and, thus, the landowning aristocracy's wealth and power.

59. A

This passage, which opens Jean-Jacques Rousseau's *The Social Contract*, most closely reflects the beliefs of the Enlightenment, choice **A**. The Enlightenment was characterized by an increasing distrust of authority and tradition, an emphasis on the powers of the individual, and a belief in logical, rational thought. Typical of Enlightenment writings, the passage uses the rhetoric of bondage and slavery to describe how human beings may free themselves from social and spiritual oppression.

60. B

The tiger that represents India, though leashed, is crouched and ready to pounce. It is glowering, and Palmerston hides behind a chair, while Campbell holds a grenade or stick. Therefore, Number I is clearly incorrect. Number II is too extreme.

61. B

The Victorian ideal for women was for them to marry, have children, and create a loving and beautiful home. Men were not expected to help with housework. While some children were tutored in the home, this was not within the scope of the ideal of domesticity, nor were the ideals concerned with the number of household members.

62. B

Romanticism is the movement that rejected the classicism of the eighteenth century and ushered in a new era of artistic freedom and creativity.

63. D

Faraday developed an electric motor and the dynamo. Koch identified the bacterium that causes tuberculosis, Nightingale pioneered clean hospitals and nurses' training, Lister encouraged the use of antiseptics, and Pasteur developed pasteurization and vaccines for rabies and anthrax.

64. C

Catherine's public endorsement of noble authority over Russian serfs aggravated the largest peasant revolt in Russian history. Peasants resented the near absolute power of the nobility over the serfs, who were usually badly treated.

65. E

The surge in population, coupled with land shortages, pushed farmers first in the Low Countries to seek innovative farming methods, which were expanded upon by English farmers, such as Charles Townsend, who invented crop rotation.

66. B

Landowners controlled Parliament in the mid to late eighteenth century. They passed laws to fence in formerly communal, village farms and created a more profit-driven farming economy that left many peasants without land to farm.

67. C

Industrialization saw the rapid growth of French and British cities. Most towns existed in the 10,000-inhabitant range, while a few urban giants of the time, such as Paris, were home to nearly one million people.

68. E

Mercantile economic practices necessitated the tight control of the economy by the government in attempting to develop a vast network of colonies from which raw materials and bullion would be collected to supply the home country's self-sustaining economy.

69. B

Utilitarianism is the belief that one's actions should be based on what provides the greatest good for the largest number of people. **A** is incorrect because utilitarianism requires laws to be evaluated according to their ability to provide the greatest good. Utilitarianism did not promote anarchy, which is described in response **C**. Utilitarianism did not disregard religion or advocate for its dissolution, though it ultimately emphasized human beings' material welfare over their spiritual condition.

70. C

In both the Fashoda incident and the Moroccan crisis, major European powers were on the brink of war. In the Fashoda incident it was Britain and France, and the Moroccan Crisis involved Germany and France.

71. A

The East India Company, a British monopoly, heralded the beginning of British domination in the subcontinent. The East India Company first became involved in India in 1691. The Seven Years' War was not fought until 1756–63, though it did help push out French interests in the region. The Sepoy rebellion was in 1857. The Mughals were defeated by East India Company forces. Tipu Sultan's loss came in 1799.

72. C

The tabular information directly supports the fact that the growing industrial employment in England was spreading beyond the base of Lancashire, as the number of workers in the industry was growing in that time frame, but the percentage of the whole workforce involved in the Lancashire cotton industry was decreasing.

73. E

The Boers despised black Africans such as Zulus and considered them to be inferior.

74. C

E is too extreme: the Decembrists wanted liberal reforms, but there is no evidence that they favored abolition of the monarchy. The Russians lost the Crimean War, and the Okhrana was the very oppressive secret police (established to look for enemies, like reformers). Pan-Slavism did become popular with many in Russia, and was not part of the

Decembrist agenda. The Decembrist revolt was an early tremor in the impending Russian Revolution, which would occur in the next century. The uprising caused Nicholas I (1825–55) to clamp down on Russia even more tightly, maintaining his autocratic control of his people and setting the stage for revolution.

75. B

Much of Baroque art in south Europe was created to fuel a resurgence in Catholic allegiance and conversions to counter the efforts of the Protestant reformers. Many artists were directly funded by the Catholic Church to produce art glorifying Catholic beliefs.

76. D

The English Civil War arose over the division between Parliament and Charles I, as they vied for dominance in English politics. Supporters of Parliament, called Roundheads, were victorious in defeating the supporters of the monarch, the Cavaliers, leading to the deposition and execution of Charles I and the establishment of the republican Commonwealth of England. The monarchy was eventually re-established in the person of Charles II, and a constitutional monarchy was created under William and Mary.

77. B

Wilhelm II saw no need to keep the Russian alliance; Russia quickly sought security in allying with France.

78. D

Bismarck's Germany saw the working class gain insurance and pensions. His need to isolate France, after the Franco-Prussian War, led to closer ties with Russia and Austria. While increasing Germany's military, he was careful not to challenge England's naval superiority. So, choice **D** is the answer.

79. D

The British specifically promised Emir Hussein ibn Ali independence in exchange for his attacking the Turks. The Armenians received no allied assistance, and the Allies did not have the means of exploiting internal social tensions. England used extensive anti-German, not anti-Turkish, propaganda. The Dardanelles were firmly controlled by the Ottoman Empire; the English tried to assault the region, but failed.

80. D

Walesa's remarkable election marked the beginning of the end of Soviet Communist domination of its Eastern European bloc of nations. His successful election inspired uprisings against Soviet-installed leaders in the other formerly controlled regions like Romania, Bulgaria, and Czechoslovakia, ultimately lifting the infamous "iron curtain."

SECTION II: FREE-RESPONSE EXPLANATIONS

Part A: Document-Based Question

Sample Essay

The 1789 meeting of the French Estates General, originally arranged to address the nation's growing economic crisis, quickly evolved into a political and social upheaval unprecedented in Europe. This effected a parallel transformation in the role of French women, previously consigned a conservative and sharply limited role. In practice, the shifts that took place in the role of women were neither as swift nor as dramatic as the broader social upheavals brought on by the demise of the existing socio-political model. Women were, however, able to substantially alter the way they were viewed by society and, perhaps more importantly, develop a nascent "feminist" lobby, campaigning for gender equality.

Contemporary documentation, such as the 1789 Petition of the Women of the Third Estate [Document 2] suggests that few women received a formal education or had either the skills or the opportunity to work outside of the home. Even wealthy or upper class women, as depicted in the 1788 Engraving About French Hairstyles [Document 1] are portrayed as objects of beauty, not as thinking individuals. The documentation does not indicate what the official response to a document such as the 1789 Petition might have been, however under the absolute rule of Louis XVI and the domination of the clergy, it would probably have been highly unusual for a woman to formally request education and increased job opportunities. Based on the events that followed, one might assume that the establishment's response, like their response to the demands of liberals in the Estates General, was inadequate.

It is possible the upper classes failed to properly appreciate the powerful ideology of the era. The Enlightenment philosophy that pervaded the intellectual output of the 18th century emphasized concepts such as the rights of man and the social contract, a government's obligation to represent its citizenry. These ideas drew the shortcomings of the French ruling classes into sharp relief and led the people to agitate for change. Arguments on human rights were easily extended, by both women and men, to address the disenfranchisement of half of France. One liberal Frenchman whose professional life would have spanned the decades leading up to the revolution wrote that it was "absurd" to clamor for the rights of men while "forgetting those rights when it comes to 12 million women. . . either no individual in mankind has true rights or all have the same ones." [Document 4] This kind of thought, shockingly liberal for the day, instilled in women a desire for equality that had not previously been given free or full expression.

Inspired by this kind of rhetoric and presented with an opportunity to effect change—thanks to surging upheavals of the revolution—French women became increasingly active in carving out a new identity and a new voice in French society.

The women depicted marching on Versailles in 1789 [Document 3], heavily armed and completely unaccompanied by men, are drawn as a highly motivated and unified mass. Female participation in the act of revolution in France demonstrated to the artist, and probably to many more, that women had strength, will, and solidarity that had not previously been demonstrated. The marching women bear as little resemblance to the timid petitioners of the Third Estate as Olympe de Gouges, daughter of a well-to-do petit bourgeois, bears to the idealized, immaculately coiffed women in the 1788 engraving [Docu-

ment 1] when she writes "all male and female citizens must contribute...to it's [the new government's] formation; it must be the same for all." [Document 7] De Gouges, who wrote the Declaration of the Right's of Women and Female Citizen in 1791, is uncompromising in her demands for gender equality. Pauline Leon, one of the organizers of the 1789 Paris bread riots, is no less vehement in her assertion that, "we are citoyennes and we cannot be indifferent to the fate of the fatherland." [Document 8]

Change, however, did not necessarily follow hot on the heels of these proclamations. As early as 1789 the National Assembly decreed that "all citizens, without distinction of birth" would be eligible for "any office or dignity." [Document 5] However, since de Gouges is still petitioning that women too must be "equally admitted to all honors, positions and public employment" [Document 7] in 1791, we must assume that although the 1789 decree granted women rights to office in principle, they were not always applied in practice. More encouraging is the 1792 divorce legislation passed by the National Assembly, [Document 8] which establishes that "divorce shall take place by mutual consent of husband and wife," establishing a degree of equality in marriage. Of course there are no documents supplied which could testify to the success or failure of the legislation.

By the time Napoleon overthrew the Directory in 1799, the Reign of Terror had already, in many ways, perverted the original ideology of the revolution. The Directory represented some attempt to restore stability and purpose to French politics, but was unstable and rife with corruption. Many of the rights established for women, notably the statute on mutually consensual divorce, were preserved in the civil sections of the Napoleonic Code, however this also enshrined the status of the husband as the head of household and in some respects, legally bound women to a subordinate status.

Still, the precedent of women's involvement at the forefront of socio-political change had been set. The anthropomorphized engraving of Equality holding a copy of the Declaration of Right's of Man and Citizen is, not insignificantly, a woman. [Document 9] Women would go on to provide some of the strongest and most enduring images of the French Revolution: the iconic Marianne, and Eugène Delacroix's Liberty, leading the people of Paris toward freedom. Practical changes came slowly over the following centuries (indeed French women did not acquire the right to vote until 1944) but the revolution nevertheless represented a watershed in terms of establishing women's interests in society and organizing a feminist voice for France.

Part B: Free-Response Question 1

Sample Essay

In early-sixteenth-century Germany, disillusionment with the governance and disseminated message of the Catholic Church spawned a new branch of Christianity in the form of Protestantism. Martin Luther is often credited for initiating the construction of this new sect of thought, but his motive was not to divorce from the Catholic Church. Rather, Luther was a dedicated Catholic who wanted to see reform realized within the Church amidst its declining social and political influence.

An ordained Catholic priest, Luther was deeply reflective, which caused him to be frustrated with his perceived inability to impact the Church's prescription for achieving the "righteousness of God" in order to gain salvation. Instead of achieving salvation through attending Mass, Luther posited in his Freedom of a Christian that man could achieve salvation through simply possessing faith in Jesus Christ. In this sense, Luther redirected the power of achieving salvation away from the controls of the Church's viceroys and toward the power of the individual believer, a primary tenet in the Protestant movement.

Another of Luther's primary concerns, as noted in his ninety-five theses nailed to the door of his Wittenberg church, was the selling of church indulgences, or ablutions from eternal punishment of sins. While the indulgences were sold to raise funds for Church expansion and construction projects, Luther thought this practice thwarted the meaning of salvation by making it a commodity for sale. He criticized this practice as straying from the teachings of Scripture, which he saw as the paramount source of truth, rather than the precedent and practice of the Church's history.

Luther's criticisms of the Church were grounded in his desire to see its reform and ultimate strengthening. His calls for secular participation in Church governance, greater recognition of the individual believer's relationship to salvation, and the discontinuation of practices he saw as corrupt were more related to his wish to see the improvement of Church policy and status within an ever-increasingly critical public. While his views became the foundation of an alternative to the Church, in the form of Protestantism, Luther was a reformer working for change within the Church; he was not working for the creation of a competing organism, which developed consequent to his influence.

Part C: Free-Response Question 2

Sample Essay

Napoleon eludes classification exclusively as a liberal or a conservative, revolutionary or reactionary. While his military conquests and liberal national policies spread social change along an axis aligned with many revolutionary ideals, his conservative governing tendencies related more to a reactionary philosophy.

Napoleon's rule affected France's legal, economic, and political institutions in ways that directly changed the French social infrastructure. Napoleon reorganized the collection of taxes in France, making them more efficient. The Bank of France was established and the French currency was strengthened. He also reorganized the departments in France and set up an efficient governing system for them. Significantly, Napoleon created the Napoleonic Code, which included the liberal provisions of equality before the law (for men) and protection of private property. Freedom of religion was permitted and jobs, even in the military, were open to those possessing the necessary talent. Additionally, many secondary schools were opened with their control moved away from the Church and into more secular hands. Universities were also strengthened. Peasants who had obtained land in the revolution were permitted to keep it, while nobles who had fled France were encouraged to return. In these ways, Napoleon demonstrated shades of liberalism and an embrace of revolutionary ideals.

Napoleon claimed to be "the revolution on horseback." Some historians have argued that his attempts to harness the revolutionary political sentiment in France were motivated purely by his own lust for power. Regardless of his motivation, he achieved many great things. By 1812 he ruled the Netherlands, Belgium, and large sections of Italy. Allied and controlled regions included the Duchy of Warsaw and most German-speaking states, Naples, and Spain. His European conquests brought huge changes socially. His policies of freedom of religion and economic equality (again, for men) were wildly received by the masses.

However, Napoleon's conquests brought much unrest throughout Europe. Such discontent and political upset within the status quo in the continental power structure challenged the conservative order in Europe. France's foreign rule encouraged nationalism throughout Europe that would live on long after Napoleon. The Holy Roman Empire finally dissolved due to his conquests, but the Napoleonic creation, the Confederation of the Rhine, would help in the unification of Germany (1871). With Napoleon's blessing, Russia was able to gain territory in Scandinavia. Many dynasties, such as the Bourbons, were forced from their thrones. Due to Napoleon's Continental System, Britain and the United States eventually went to war (this war became known as the War of 1812), and Napoleon's sale of the Louisiana Territory laid the foundation for the United States to become a world power. The French defeat at the Battle of Trafalgar confirmed Britain's naval dominance in Europe, but the cost in human lives and money was enormous. After Napoleon's final defeat in 1815, the Congress of Vienna restored the ousted ruling families. These families sought to reestablish absolutism and remove any traces of Napoleon's liberal policies. This led to dozens of revolts and revolutions across Europe for the next fifty years.

Despite his liberal actions, Napoleon also had a conservative side. Under his rule, women lost many of the rights they had gained in the French Revolution. Men were the absolute heads of their households—though divorce was still permitted—and women had very limited control over property. Freedom of expression was very limited and police informants kept track of malcontents. Political dissent was not freely allowed and suspects could be questioned and detained by the police. Napoleon made peace with the Catholic Church, though he still maintained a degree of control over the church in France. Though France had a constitution and plebiscites were conducted, in reality Napoleon was an absolute ruler. In this way, he was the head of a conservative type of government.

In conclusion, Napoleon's rule was certainly complex. Because of this complexity, he was not singly revolutionary or reactionary, liberal or conservative. Ultimately, Napoleon was politically conservative, but embraced many liberal socioeconomic ideals. Napoleon's policies and philosophy seem to fit into more of a hybrid of such classifications, making him nonetheless powerful in the effect he had on the direction of European history.

PRACTICE EXAM 2

AP EUROPEAN HISTORY PRACTICE EXAM 2 ANSWER SHEET

1. Ⓐ Ⓑ Ⓒ Ⓓ Ⓔ	21. Ⓐ Ⓑ Ⓒ Ⓓ Ⓔ	41. Ⓐ Ⓑ Ⓒ Ⓓ Ⓔ	61. Ⓐ Ⓑ Ⓒ Ⓓ Ⓔ
2. Ⓐ Ⓑ Ⓒ Ⓓ Ⓔ	22. Ⓐ Ⓑ Ⓒ Ⓓ Ⓔ	42. Ⓐ Ⓑ Ⓒ Ⓓ Ⓔ	62. Ⓐ Ⓑ Ⓒ Ⓓ Ⓔ
3. Ⓐ Ⓑ Ⓒ Ⓓ Ⓔ	23. Ⓐ Ⓑ Ⓒ Ⓓ Ⓔ	43. Ⓐ Ⓑ Ⓒ Ⓓ Ⓔ	63. Ⓐ Ⓑ Ⓒ Ⓓ Ⓔ
4. Ⓐ Ⓑ Ⓒ Ⓓ Ⓔ	24. Ⓐ Ⓑ Ⓒ Ⓓ Ⓔ	44. Ⓐ Ⓑ Ⓒ Ⓓ Ⓔ	64. Ⓐ Ⓑ Ⓒ Ⓓ Ⓔ
5. Ⓐ Ⓑ Ⓒ Ⓓ Ⓔ	25. Ⓐ Ⓑ Ⓒ Ⓓ Ⓔ	45. Ⓐ Ⓑ Ⓒ Ⓓ Ⓔ	65. Ⓐ Ⓑ Ⓒ Ⓓ Ⓔ
6. Ⓐ Ⓑ Ⓒ Ⓓ Ⓔ	26. Ⓐ Ⓑ Ⓒ Ⓓ Ⓔ	46. Ⓐ Ⓑ Ⓒ Ⓓ Ⓔ	66. Ⓐ Ⓑ Ⓒ Ⓓ Ⓔ
7. Ⓐ Ⓑ Ⓒ Ⓓ Ⓔ	27. Ⓐ Ⓑ Ⓒ Ⓓ Ⓔ	47. Ⓐ Ⓑ Ⓒ Ⓓ Ⓔ	67. Ⓐ Ⓑ Ⓒ Ⓓ Ⓔ
8. Ⓐ Ⓑ Ⓒ Ⓓ Ⓔ	28. Ⓐ Ⓑ Ⓒ Ⓓ Ⓔ	48. Ⓐ Ⓑ Ⓒ Ⓓ Ⓔ	68. Ⓐ Ⓑ Ⓒ Ⓓ Ⓔ
9. Ⓐ Ⓑ Ⓒ Ⓓ Ⓔ	29. Ⓐ Ⓑ Ⓒ Ⓓ Ⓔ	49. Ⓐ Ⓑ Ⓒ Ⓓ Ⓔ	69. Ⓐ Ⓑ Ⓒ Ⓓ Ⓔ
10. Ⓐ Ⓑ Ⓒ Ⓓ Ⓔ	30. Ⓐ Ⓑ Ⓒ Ⓓ Ⓔ	50. Ⓐ Ⓑ Ⓒ Ⓓ Ⓔ	70. Ⓐ Ⓑ Ⓒ Ⓓ Ⓔ
11. Ⓐ Ⓑ Ⓒ Ⓓ Ⓔ	31. Ⓐ Ⓑ Ⓒ Ⓓ Ⓔ	51. Ⓐ Ⓑ Ⓒ Ⓓ Ⓔ	71. Ⓐ Ⓑ Ⓒ Ⓓ Ⓔ
12. Ⓐ Ⓑ Ⓒ Ⓓ Ⓔ	32. Ⓐ Ⓑ Ⓒ Ⓓ Ⓔ	52. Ⓐ Ⓑ Ⓒ Ⓓ Ⓔ	72. Ⓐ Ⓑ Ⓒ Ⓓ Ⓔ
13. Ⓐ Ⓑ Ⓒ Ⓓ Ⓔ	33. Ⓐ Ⓑ Ⓒ Ⓓ Ⓔ	53. Ⓐ Ⓑ Ⓒ Ⓓ Ⓔ	73. Ⓐ Ⓑ Ⓒ Ⓓ Ⓔ
14. Ⓐ Ⓑ Ⓒ Ⓓ Ⓔ	34. Ⓐ Ⓑ Ⓒ Ⓓ Ⓔ	54. Ⓐ Ⓑ Ⓒ Ⓓ Ⓔ	74. Ⓐ Ⓑ Ⓒ Ⓓ Ⓔ
15. Ⓐ Ⓑ Ⓒ Ⓓ Ⓔ	35. Ⓐ Ⓑ Ⓒ Ⓓ Ⓔ	55. Ⓐ Ⓑ Ⓒ Ⓓ Ⓔ	75. Ⓐ Ⓑ Ⓒ Ⓓ Ⓔ
16. Ⓐ Ⓑ Ⓒ Ⓓ Ⓔ	36. Ⓐ Ⓑ Ⓒ Ⓓ Ⓔ	56. Ⓐ Ⓑ Ⓒ Ⓓ Ⓔ	76. Ⓐ Ⓑ Ⓒ Ⓓ Ⓔ
17. Ⓐ Ⓑ Ⓒ Ⓓ Ⓔ	37. Ⓐ Ⓑ Ⓒ Ⓓ Ⓔ	57. Ⓐ Ⓑ Ⓒ Ⓓ Ⓔ	77. Ⓐ Ⓑ Ⓒ Ⓓ Ⓔ
18. Ⓐ Ⓑ Ⓒ Ⓓ Ⓔ	38. Ⓐ Ⓑ Ⓒ Ⓓ Ⓔ	58. Ⓐ Ⓑ Ⓒ Ⓓ Ⓔ	78. Ⓐ Ⓑ Ⓒ Ⓓ Ⓔ
19. Ⓐ Ⓑ Ⓒ Ⓓ Ⓔ	39. Ⓐ Ⓑ Ⓒ Ⓓ Ⓔ	59. Ⓐ Ⓑ Ⓒ Ⓓ Ⓔ	79. Ⓐ Ⓑ Ⓒ Ⓓ Ⓔ
20. Ⓐ Ⓑ Ⓒ Ⓓ Ⓔ	40. Ⓐ Ⓑ Ⓒ Ⓓ Ⓔ	60. Ⓐ Ⓑ Ⓒ Ⓓ Ⓔ	80. Ⓐ Ⓑ Ⓒ Ⓓ Ⓔ

AP EUROPEAN HISTORY

Three hours and 5 minutes are allotted for this examination: 55 minutes for Section I, which consists of multiple-choice questions, and 130 minutes for Section II, which consists of essay questions. 15 minutes of Section II are devoted to a mandatory reading period, primarily for the document-based essay question in Part A. Section I is printed in this examination booklet. Section II is printed in a separate booklet. In determining your grade, the two sections are given equal weight.

SECTION I

Time—55 minutes
Number of questions—80
Percent of total grade—50

Section I of this examination contains 80 multiple-choice questions. Therefore, please be careful to fill in only the ovals that are preceded by numbers 1 through 80 on your answer sheet.

General Instructions

DO NOT OPEN THIS BOOKLET UNTIL YOU ARE INSTRUCTED TO DO SO.

INDICATE YOUR ANSWERS TO QUESTIONS IN SECTION I ON THE SEPARATE ANSWER SHEET ENCLOSED. No credit will be given for anything written in this examination booklet, but you may use the booklet for notes or scratchwork. After you have decided which of the suggested answers is best, COMPLETELY fill in the corresponding oval on the answer sheet. Give only one answer to each question. If you change an answer, be sure that the previous mark is erased completely.

Example   Sample Answer

Chicago is a

   (A) state
   (B) continent
   (C) country
   (D) city
   (E) village

Many candidates wonder whether or not to guess the answers to questions about which they are not certain. In this section of the examination, as a correction for haphazard guessing, one-fourth of the number of questions you answer incorrectly will be subtracted from the number of questions you answer correctly. It is improbable, therefore, that mere guessing will improve your score significantly; it may even lower your score, and it does take time. If, however, you are not sure of the best answer but have some knowledge of the question and are able to eliminate one or more of the answer choices as wrong, your chance of answering correctly is improved, and it may be to your advantage to answer such a question.

Use your time effectively, working as rapidly as you can without losing accuracy. Do not spend too much time on questions that are too difficult. Go on to other questions and come back to the difficult ones later if you have time. It is not expected that everyone will be able to answer the multiple-choice questions.

Directions: Each of the questions or incomplete statements below is followed by five suggested answers or completions. Select the one that is best in each case and then fill in the corresponding oval on the answer sheet.

1. Historian Jacob Burckhardt's view of the Renaissance is often criticized by other historians for

   (A) overemphasizing the importance of the early Middle Ages
   (B) discounting the influence of religion in creating the Renaissance epoch
   (C) overstating the uniqueness of the Renaissance as a "rebirth"
   (D) overlooking the role of the peasant class in driving the Renaissance
   (E) characterizing the Renaissance as being primarily an economic innovation

2. Which of the following were factors in the start of the Hundred Years' War (1337–1453)?

   I.   Rivalry of England and France as the two strongest Western European powers
   II. The land held by English kings in southwestern France
   III. Manufacture of woolen textiles in Flanders
   IV. The English king's claim to the French throne

   (A) I and II
   (B) I, III, and IV
   (C) II and III
   (D) I and IV
   (E) I, II, III, and IV

3. The Tudor line of English monarchs established a tradition of

   (A) absolute rule
   (B) parliamentary supremacy
   (C) constitutional rule
   (D) mercantilism
   (E) excessive imperial spending

4. The Hundred Years' War settled the question of

   (A) whether England was to retain continental possessions in France
   (B) whether France would claim the English throne
   (C) whether France would remain absolutist in its government model
   (D) whether Catholicism or Protestantism would dominate in England
   (E) whether the Lancasters or Yorks would rule England

5. Which ruler is credited with establishing a strengthened, consolidated monarchy, thus becoming the "founder of French absolutism"?

   (A) Charles VIII
   (B) Louis XIV
   (C) Elizabeth I
   (D) Louis XI
   (E) Philip VI

GO ON TO THE NEXT PAGE

AP EUROPEAN HISTORY MULTIPLE-CHOICE QUESTIONS

6. Which of the following were tactics used by Ferdinand and Isabella of Spain?

    I.   Directly limiting the constitutions of Aragon and Castile to enhance their power

    II.   Forcing the expulsion or forced conversion of non-Catholics

    III. Pursuing an aggressive policy in acquiring Italian lands

    IV. Increasing political decentralization and fragmentation toward a confederate state structure

(A) I and III
(B) I, II, and IV
(C) II and III
(D) II only
(E) I, II, III, and IV

7. All of the following were factors undermining the influence of the Catholic Church in the later Middle Ages EXCEPT

(A) an increase of nationalism
(B) the rise of strong monarchs in England and France
(C) the new economic emphasis on money
(D) the growth of humanism
(E) groups such as the Franciscans

8. Francesco Petrarch is most closely associated with which of the following?

(A) laissez-faire economics
(B) humanism
(C) the Price Revolution
(D) the Council of Trent
(E) naturalism

GO ON TO THE NEXT PAGE

© Art Resource

9.   Jan van Eyck's painting, shown above, represents the Renaissance in Flanders because

(A) its attention to details increases its realism, the staple of Flemish Renaissance art
(B) its focus on religion makes it uniquely Flemish
(C) its inclusion of a pregnant woman indicates a rebirth, which was a primary characteristic of Renaissance Flemish art
(D) its sentimentality and anecdotal style typifies the Flemish Renaissance style
(E) A and D

GO ON TO THE NEXT PAGE

AP EUROPEAN HISTORY MULTIPLE-CHOICE QUESTIONS

10. One direct effect the Black Death had on the Church was that the Black Death

    (A) led to an increase in the proportion of unqualified clergy
    (B) reduced the percentage of corrupt Church leaders
    (C) permanently discontinued the sale of indulgences
    (D) intensified national opposition to the Avignon Papacy
    (E) caused a resurgence of holy crusades

11. All of the following were reasons the Protestant Reformation of the sixteenth century was successful EXCEPT

    (A) kings wanted to obtain absolute control within their realms and targeted weakening the Church
    (B) there existed a land-hungry nobility that sought possession of Church property
    (C) there existed a rising middle class alienated from the Church's teachings
    (D) the Renaissance heralded a spirit of questioning and individualism
    (E) the German provinces were united under a strong monarch who was opposed to the Church

12. The development of the absolute state is related to the Protestant Reformation because

    (A) Martin Luther advocated for an absolute state
    (B) the Church universally favored absolutism
    (C) the Protestant movement inherently opposed absolutism
    (D) the division of political and religious authority had formerly weakened the power of the political ruler
    (E) the primary base of support for Protestantism came from the peasant class

13. Which of the following were concepts raised in Martin Luther's protesting beliefs?

    (A) The assertion of papal fallibility
    (B) A proclamation that Jan Hus's doctrines were not heretical
    (C) An attack on the Church's sale of indulgences
    (D) The assertion that salvation could be achieved through faith alone
    (E) All of the above

14. Which of the following was invented at the end of the fifteenth century in Germany?

    (A) Algebra
    (B) The printing press
    (C) The steam-powered motor
    (D) Division of labor
    (E) The smelting process

15. Ulrich Zwingli's teachings agreed with Martin Luther's on all of the following EXCEPT

    (A) the meaning of Communion
    (B) salvation by faith alone
    (C) involving more laity in Church governance
    (D) the need for reform in the Church
    (E) denouncing the sale of indulgences

16. Which of the following is true of Philip II of Spain's reign?

    (A) He resolved the economic problems in Spain.
    (B) He implemented reforms tolerating religious diversity.
    (C) His military attacks ended Turkish control of the Mediterranean.
    (D) He successfully ended the independence movement in the Low Countries.
    (E) He avoided conflict with England.

17. All of the following were principal motives for European colonization in the fifteenth and sixteenth centuries EXCEPT

    (A) the Renaissance spirit of embracing adventure
    (B) the desire to spread Christianity
    (C) the quest for natural resources
    (D) the need for outside markets
    (E) overcrowding due to industrial agglomeration

18. The Thirty Years' War was significant in

    (A) developing a more modern state system
    (B) aiding in the breakup of the Holy Roman Empire
    (C) moving the focus of economic wealth from central to western Europe
    (D) promoting greater religious diversity in Europe
    (E) all of the above

GO ON TO THE NEXT PAGE

19. Henry IV of France embarked on a foreign policy focused primarily on

    (A) preventing Hapsburg encirclement of France
    (B) containing Elizabeth I of England
    (C) obtaining control of the English Channel
    (D) fortifying the Franco-Spanish border
    (E) conquering non-Catholic nations

20. Cardinal Mazarin of France was instrumental in

    (A) building enthusiasm for a parliamentary democracy in France
    (B) regaining public support for the Crown
    (C) establishing a legacy of absolutism
    (D) reducing the tax burden on the French people
    (E) creating a system of justice in France

21. Under Louis XIV, the Privy Council controlled

    (A) religious matters
    (B) issues of international policy
    (C) finance and war
    (D) the newspapers
    (E) legal cases

22. Which of the following was not a provision in the Treaty of Utrecht (1713)?

    (A) The French and Spanish thrones were to remain permanently separated.
    (B) Spain was permitted to maintain its control of Gibraltar.
    (C) The duchies of Prussia and Savoy were transformed into kingdoms.
    (D) The Dutch were allowed to build and maintain fortresses along their frontier.
    (E) France recognized the English Hanoverian succession.

23. The English conflict between King James I and Parliament was a struggle involving all of the following EXCEPT

    (A) the theory of the supremacy of common law versus the Stuarts' divine-right theory
    (B) the focus on taxation
    (C) Catholics versus Protestants
    (D) James's anti-Spanish policy
    (E) the Magna Carta

24. "Tyranny is the exercise of power beyond right, which nobody can have a right to; and this is making use of the power any one has in his hands, not for the good of those who are under it, but for his own private, separate advantage."

    The quotation above is a formulation of the ideas of

    (A) Thomas Hobbes
    (B) Jean Jacques Rousseau
    (C) Fredrick Engels
    (D) Jeremy Bentham
    (E) John Locke

25. Who is credited with popularizing the idea that valid knowledge could be discovered from sensory experience and observation, i.e., the foundation of the scientific method?

    (A) William Gilbert
    (B) Robert Boyle
    (C) Francis Bacon
    (D) Tycho Brahe
    (E) Rene Descartes

GO ON TO THE NEXT PAGE

© Art Resource

26. The above artwork is most associated with which movement in painting?

(A) Neoclassicism
(B) Dadaism
(C) Rococo
(D) Realism
(E) Baroque

GO ON TO THE NEXT PAGE

27. The Hohenzollerns of Prussia between the reigns of Frederick William, the Great Elector, and Frederick the Great are best known for

    (A) unifying the fractured German lands into a stronger Prussian state
    (B) destroying the financial stability of the Prussian economy
    (C) weakening the Prussian tradition of a strong military
    (D) abolishing the graduated income tax in Prussia
    (E) granting the local provinces greater autonomy

28. Catherine II of Russia and Frederick II of Prussia were similar in that they both

    (A) pursued strengthening absolute rule over their subjects
    (B) forced conversion to Catholicism within their realms
    (C) pursued a foreign policy of isolationism
    (D) yielded greater autonomy to Poland
    (E) failed to designate a clear successor, thereby causing chaos upon their deaths

29. Which of the following artists worked in the Impressionist style?

    (A) Claude Monet
    (B) Pablo Picasso
    (C) Théodore Géricault
    (D) René Magritte
    (E) Eugène Delacroix

30. The English "South Sea Bubble" refers to

    (A) the inflated confidence in a British corporation of investors that collapsed
    (B) a slave-trade triangle from Africa to South America
    (C) a banking explosion that caused stock prices to soar
    (D) Robert Walpole's economic policy
    (E) the primary area explored by British merchants

31. During the nineteenth century in Europe there were major outbreaks of revolution in which of the following areas?

    I. France
    II. Austria-Hungary
    III. Prussia
    IV. Spain

    (A) I and II
    (B) I and IV
    (C) I, II, and IV
    (D) I, II, and III
    (E) I, II, III, and IV

32. All of the following are examples of nineteenth-century British imperial policy EXCEPT

    (A) extending Britain's involvement in slave trading
    (B) expanding British control in southern Africa
    (C) establishing trading posts in India
    (D) opening China to Western trade
    (E) promoting the sale of opium in China

33. Which of the following contributed to European territorial expansion in the nineteenth century?

    I. Steam-powered ships
    II. Medical advancements
    III. Improved weapons, such as the Maxim gun
    IV. Nationalist movements in Western Europe

    (A) I and II
    (B) II and III
    (C) III and IV
    (D) I, II, and III
    (E) I, II, III, and IV

34. The purpose of the British North American Act was to

    (A) challenge Spanish holdings in the South and West
    (B) disrupt French exploration along the Mississippi
    (C) allow Canada to administer its own affairs
    (D) attempt to limit French influence in Quebec
    (E) formalize relations between the colony of Canada and the United States

GO ON TO THE NEXT PAGE

AP EUROPEAN HISTORY MULTIPLE-CHOICE QUESTIONS

35. Causes of the Sepoy Rebellion included all of the following EXCEPT

 (A) Indian suspicions that the British wanted to stifle native religions
 (B) rumors that claimed rifle cartridges contained animal fats
 (C) British efforts to eliminate *sati*
 (D) Queen Victoria's claims to be Empress of India
 (E) Indian nationalism and objections to Britain's annexing territory

36. The notion that the English had adopted responsible government because their northern climate made them enthusiastic and hearty is most associated with

 (A) John Locke
 (B) Baron de Montesquieu
 (C) George Whitefield
 (D) Charles Wesley
 (E) Jean Jacques Rousseau

37. Russian nineteenth-century foreign policy centered around all of the following EXCEPT

 (A) concerns about the goals of the Dual Monarchy
 (B) annexation of Asian territory
 (C) warm-water ports and access to the Mediterranean
 (D) attempts to annex Japanese-held islands
 (E) establishing colonies in North Africa

38. The nineteenth-century British Liberal and Conservative parties had which of the following in common?

 (A) Both supported home rule for Ireland.
 (B) Both supported reducing British military responses abroad.
 (C) Both enacted legislation expanding suffrage for men.
 (D) Both favored women's suffrage.
 (E) Neither wished to cooperate with the American opening of Japanese ports.

39. In literature, music, and the visual arts, idealizing nature, personal freedom, and the exotic were all characteristics of

 (A) Impressionism
 (B) Expressionism
 (C) Realism
 (D) Romanticism
 (E) Classicism

40. By 1911, which of the following British institution's power was permanently reduced?

 (A) The House of Lords
 (B) The monarchy
 (C) Coalition governments
 (D) The Labour Party
 (E) The Liberal Party

41. The purpose of *Kulturkampf* was to

 (A) isolate the Junkers politically
 (B) promote the power of the Reichstag
 (C) put allegiance to Prussia above Catholicism
 (D) bring universal suffrage to the Prussian upper house
 (E) encourage the development of Prussia's socialist movement

42. The 1861 Emancipation Edict in Russia

 (A) allowed serfs independence from the landowning nobles, but kept them tied to their villages
 (B) allowed nobles to restructure payments for serfs to buy titles
 (C) reformed the number of taxes serfs had to pay
 (D) reduced by half the number of days peasants were required to work for the landlords
 (E) allowed the imperial government to annex unused lands

43. The People's Will is associated with which of the following?

 (A) The 1825 Decembrist revolt
 (B) The assassination of Czar Alexander II
 (C) The assassination of Peter Stolypin
 (D) Dismantling the Okhrana
 (E) A and D

44. The religious movement known as Deism was

 (A) a reaction to the wars of religion
 (B) prompted by a desire to subject religion to the scientific processes
 (C) an attempt at emphasizing the role of reason in finding truth
 (D) created to develop a religion all humankind could accept without controversy
 (E) all of the above

GO ON TO THE NEXT PAGE

AP EUROPEAN HISTORY MULTIPLE-CHOICE QUESTIONS

45. When the Austrian Prince Metternich referred to Italy as "a geographical expression," he meant which of the following?

    (A) Italy had attempted to expand into Austrian territory.
    (B) Italy's geographic location was advantageous to Austria.
    (C) There was no political entity that could correctly be called Italy.
    (D) Italy was incapable of ever unifying.
    (E) Austria was violently opposed to Italian unification.

46. The Women's Social and Political Union gained political and social attention when it began

    (A) supporting David Lloyd George over Herbert Asquith
    (B) using radical and sometimes violent tactics
    (C) protesting against the British monarchy
    (D) combining forces with the American suffrage movement
    (E) encouraging hunger strikes in all women's prisons

47. The nineteenth-century idea of compulsory conscription was first realized in

    (A) France
    (B) Great Britain
    (C) Russia
    (D) Germany
    (E) Italy

48. Great Britain entered World War I in 1914 after which of the following events?

    (A) Russian troops were mobilized.
    (B) German troops overran France's eastern boundary.
    (C) Austria-Hungary's delivered an ultimatum to Serbia.
    (D) Serbia requested British military support.
    (E) Germany invaded neutral Belgium.

49. The Fourteen Points can best be described as

    (A) Woodrow Wilson's idealistic goals for the postwar world
    (B) the actual framework for the Treaty of Versailles
    (C) America's attempt to trick Germany into surrender
    (D) an American effort to appease French political interests
    (E) an attempt to pacify the American public during a tumultuous time period

50. Which of the following actions, undertaken by Germany in the early twentieth century, signaled the outbreak of World War II?

    (A) The Anschluss
    (B) Annexation of the Sudetenland
    (C) The invasion of Poland by Germany
    (D) The Munich Pact
    (E) Moving German troops into the Rhineland

51. The year 1941 was a critical point in World War II because

    (A) Germany began its assault on the USSR
    (B) France surrendered to Germany
    (C) the RAF received American bombers
    (D) Japan attacked the United States
    (E) A and D

52. The purpose of the Nuremberg Laws was to

    (A) make labor unions illegal in Germany
    (B) unite Austrian and German military forces
    (C) isolate and disenfranchise Germany's Jews
    (D) consolidate Nazi control over public schools
    (E) limit the independence of the Catholic Church in Germany

53. Which of the following are true of the Marshall Plan?

    I.   It promised extensive financial aid to European nations.
    II. It was sponsored by the United States.
    III. Nations receiving aid had to pledge cooperation.
    IV. It refused aid to Soviet-held nations.

    (A) II and III
    (B) III and IV
    (C) I, II, and III
    (D) II, III, and IV
    (E) I, II, III, and IV

54. Walter Ulbricht is most closely associated with which of the following?

    (A) Establishing a strong Communist force in East Germany.
    (B) An effort to defy the Italian attempt to make East Germany a Soviet satellite.
    (C) Encouraging Czechoslovakia to remain under Soviet domination.
    (D) Helping Marshall Tito gain power in Yugoslavia.
    (E) Helping Stalin establish stronger ties in Austria.

GO ON TO THE NEXT PAGE

58

AP EUROPEAN HISTORY MULTIPLE-CHOICE QUESTIONS

55. The purpose of the Bretton Woods Conference was to

 (A) isolate the Soviet Union by trade embargoes
 (B) help promote economic stability in the post–World War II era
 (C) help the United Nations to build its security forces
 (D) announce the beginning of the Truman Doctrine
 (E) end American financial and military influence in Western Europe

56. France quit their colonial efforts in Indochina in 1954 when

 (A) it lost the battle at Dien Bien Phu
 (B) America withdrew its support of France
 (C) China threatened to aid the Viet Minh
 (D) the Korean War ended without a clear western victory
 (E) Stalin threatened to train Vietnamese troops

57. The Soviet blockade of West Berlin led to

 (A) decreased numbers of British and French forces in West Germany
 (B) the building of the Berlin Wall
 (C) the creation of NATO
 (D) the creation of the Warsaw Pact
 (E) the end of the Marshall Plan

58. A military coalition of which of the following nations briefly recaptured the Egyptian-held Suez Canal in 1956?

 I. Israel
 II. United States
 III. France
 IV. Britain

 (A) I and II
 (B) II and IV
 (C) I, II, and III
 (D) I, III, and IV
 (E) I, II, III, and IV

59. In October, 1957, the USSR shocked and alarmed the West when

 (A) Khruschev ordered Soviet troops into Hungary
 (B) *Sputnik* was launched
 (C) Khruschev sent troops to Cuba
 (D) the Soviets openly criticized Marshall Tito
 (E) the USSR offered to broker a nonproliferation treaty

60. The Sino-Soviet split in the early 1960s essentially was over

 (A) the Soviets' refusal to help China develop nuclear power
 (B) China's opposition to the USSR's increasing hostility against the United States
 (C) the USSR's refusal to continue sending financial support to North Vietnam
 (D) philosophical disputes about the meaning and path of Communist expansion
 (E) China's economic crisis when the Great Leap Forward failed

61. One of the underlying causes of the storming of the Bastille occurred when

 (A) Louis XVI attempted to escape to Austria
 (B) Marquis de Lafayette was unable to keep his forces loyal
 (C) Louis XVI ordered his Swiss guard to march on Paris and reinforce the Bastille
 (D) extremely radical elements in the Estates-General revolted
 (E) Louis XVI dismissed his finance minister, Jacques Necker

62. The effects of the Dreyfus case in late-nineteenth-century France signaled which of the following?

 (A) A long-lasting political divide between the liberal and conservative thinkers in France that weakened the Third Republic until its defeat by Germany in 1940
 (B) A unification of the pro- and anti-imperialists in France
 (C) The calming of the hysteric, mob-based tendencies of the French Revolution
 (D) A call for greater tolerance of French Protestants
 (E) A and D

63. Alexander II of Russia is associated with all of the following EXCEPT

 (A) reforming serfdom practices
 (B) improving the army
 (C) reorganizing the judicial system
 (D) "Russifying" Poland
 (E) pacifying revolutionaries

GO ON TO THE NEXT PAGE

64. Both Friedrich Nietzsche and Sigmund Freud

    (A) discounted the sole importance of rationality and reason
    (B) attacked the role of emotions in finding truth
    (C) explained human behavior psychoanalytically
    (D) focused on the interplay between Christianity and truth
    (E) aligned with the Romantic movement in explaining reality

65. Which of the following was not a potential factor in the outbreak of World War I?

    (A) Bismarck's dismissal by William II of Germany
    (B) Serb nationalism
    (C) imperialistic competition in Africa
    (D) Moroccan independence
    (E) British support of Ottoman dominance in the Middle East

66. Vladimir Lenin's vision for a socialist state differed from that of other leading Russian and German Marxists in that

    (A) he criticized labor unions for their focus on short-term goals rather than a long-term commitment to revolutionary change
    (B) he rejected the notion of an undemocratically formed revolutionary party
    (C) he insisted that revolution would come through social change over time
    (D) he focused on the workers rather than the ruling elite
    (E) he held views more moderate in nature than the Mensheviks' ideas

67. Reasons for American entry in World War I included which of the following?

    I.   Britain exaggerated stories of German atrocities against civilians.
    II. The Germans followed a policy of unrestricted submarine warfare.
    III. The Zimmerman telegram angered Americans.
    IV. British officials were engaged in bribing high-ranking American officials.

    (A) I and IV
    (B) II and III
    (C) I, II, and IV
    (D) I, II, and III
    (E) I, II, III, and IV

68. Which of the following statements regarding the opening months of World War I is accurate?

    (A) German Socialist parties violently protested involvement in the war.
    (B) French liberals sought to overthrow the Third Republic.
    (C) Britain's recruiting efforts were hindered because of strong political ties with Germany.
    (D) Nations involved were enthusiastic and optimistic regarding a quick victory.
    (E) Britain and France actively sought to end American neutrality.

69. The Russian provisional government of Kerensky failed in part because

    (A) it refused to allow military personnel to vote
    (B) women were not given full rights
    (C) Stalin would not support Kerensky
    (D) it continued Russia's participation in World War I
    (E) Czar Nicholas refused to acknowledge Kerensky's right to rule

70. The NEP (New Economic Policy) is best described as

    (A) Stalin's attempt to isolate rebellious peasant factions and force them into collectives
    (B) Trotsky's economic policy to promote heavy industry
    (C) Lenin's program to appease peasants and increase agricultural production
    (D) Lenin and Trotsky's economic program to increase production of consumer goods
    (E) the Bolsheviks' "war communism" policy

71. The Lateran Pact of 1929 resulted in

    (A) a virtual alliance between the Catholic Church and Mussolini
    (B) Pope Pius XI's tentative cooperation with Hitler
    (C) the Catholic Church's condemnation of Communist policies
    (D) the Catholic Church's opposition to fascist ideology
    (E) Pope Pius XI's ceding Vatican lands to Mussolini

GO ON TO THE NEXT PAGE

AP EUROPEAN HISTORY MULTIPLE-CHOICE QUESTIONS

72. Which of the following is true regarding the Beer Hall Putsch?

    (A) It eliminated General Ludendorf from German politics.
    (B) It provided the basis for a political alliance between Hitler and General Hindenburg.
    (C) Many high-ranking Communists were killed in the failed coup.
    (D) It provided Hitler with a political forum through which to popularize his ideology.
    (E) The Nazi Party was banned from German politics.

73. Neville Chamberlain's "peace in our time" comments were made in regard to

    (A) the Munich Pact
    (B) the Rome-Berlin Axis
    (C) the Ribbentrop-Molotov Agreement
    (D) the Treaty of Locarno
    (E) the Kellogg-Briand Pact

74. A speechwriter for Adolf Hitler most likely would have addressed which of the following topics?

    I.   Harsh criticism of the Treaty of Versailles
    II. Promoting the economic status of working women
    III. Criticism of the Weimar Republic
    IV. Praise for German nationalism
    V.   Promises to increase employment

    (A) I and II
    (B) I and IV
    (C) I, II, and III
    (D) III, IV, and V
    (E) I, III, IV, and V

75. The goal of Germany's Operation Barbarossa was

    (A) the quick defeat of Britain by Germany
    (B) the elimination of Poland's intellectual elites
    (C) a decisive surprise attack against the USSR
    (D) to keep the United States neutral
    (E) to shore up Italy's attacks against the Suez Canal

76. The Truman Doctrine was the American response to

    (A) the rise of communism in China
    (B) the rise of communism in the Caribbean
    (C) the communist takeover of Greece
    (D) the attempted Soviet expansion in Eastern Europe
    (E) French aggression in Indochina

77. The Soviet leader who first denounced the abuses of Stalin was

    (A) Nikita Khruschev
    (B) Yuri Andropov
    (C) Boris Yeltsin
    (D) Leonid Brezhnev
    (E) Mikhail Gorbachev

78. All of the following are true of the Weimar constitution in Germany EXCEPT

    (A) it guaranteed universal suffrage
    (B) it instituted direct election for the Reichstag and the president
    (C) it allowed for a temporary presidential dictatorship
    (D) it made seats in the Reichstag accessible to small, minority parties
    (E) it called for the suspension of religious tolerance

79. The 1933 Reichstag fire was a turning point in Hitler's rise to power for what reason?

    (A) The fire created public outrage toward German Jews, thereby allowing for greater public acceptance of Hitler's racist ideas.
    (B) It allowed for Hitler to prey upon the German fear of communist infiltration, thereby increasing public acceptance of his suspension of civil liberties.
    (C) It increased hatred of Britain and its allies.
    (D) The fire worsened the depressive economic cycle in Germany.
    (E) The fire killed many of Hitler's main political opponents.

80. Pablo Picasso's *Guernica* (1937) was most influenced by which of the following events?

    (A) The German invasion of Czechoslovakia
    (B) Mussolini's rise to power in Italy
    (C) Stalin's purges
    (D) The Cold War
    (E) The Spanish Civil War

IF YOU FINISH BEFORE YOUR TIME IS CALLED, YOU MAY CHECK YOUR WORK ON THIS SECTION. DO NOT GO ON TO SECTION II UNTIL YOU ARE TOLD TO DO SO.

END OF SECTION I

AP EUROPEAN HISTORY
SECTION II
Part A

(Suggested planning and writing time—45 minutes)
Percent of Section II score—45

<u>Directions:</u> The following question is based on the accompanying Documents 1–11.

This question is designed to test your ability to work with historical documents. As you analyze the documents, <u>take into account both the sources of the documents and the authors' points of view</u>. Write an essay on the following topic that integrates your analysis of the documents. **Do not simply summarize the documents individually**. You may refer to relevant historical facts and developments not mentioned in the documents

1. Historians refer to the young generation that fought in World War I as the "Lost Generation." Using these documents, evaluate the meaning and veracity of this label.

Historical Background: World War I was fought from 1914–18 and concluded with the signing of treaties in 1919. The catalyst that began the war was the assassination of Austrian Archduke Franz Ferdinand in Sarajevo by Serbian nationalists. What resulted was an escalation in tension and hostility between European nations that resulted in a bloody outcome. While most Europeans believed this crisis would be solved diplomatically, the allure of war and unwillingness to compromise resulted in a devastating conflict. Because of modern weapons, the war that ensued was one of the most destructive in European history and involved both civilians and soldiers. Like most wars, it was fought largely by those between the ages of 17–25.

Document 1

> Our hearts beat with enthusiasm. A kind of intoxication takes possession of us…Women hold up
> their children. We are carried away by the greeting of the land, the mystery that the future holds,
> the thought of glorious adventure, and the pride of being chosen to share it.
> —Andre Friborg; France, 1914

Document 2

> There was only one topic of conversation—war. The supporters of war seem to be in a great majority.
> Were these pugnacious fellows, young and old, bereft of their senses? Were they so ignorant of the
> horrors of war?…Vast crowds of demonstrators paraded…Patriotic demonstrations had an
> intoxicating effect and excited the war-mongers to excess.
> —Philip Scheidemann (1865–1939)

GO ON TO THE NEXT PAGE

Document 3

…The first shock at the news of war—the war that no one, people or government, had wanted—the war which had slipped, much against their will, out of the clumsy hands of the diplomats who had been bluffing and toying with it, had suddenly been transformed into enthusiasm. There were parades in the street, flags, ribbons, and music burst forth everywhere, young recruits were marching triumphantly, their faces lighting up at the cheering—they, the John Does and Richard Roes who usually go unnoticed and uncelebrated…I must acknowledge that there was a majestic, rapturous, and even seductive something in this first outbreak of the people from which one could escape only with difficulty and in spite of all my hatred and diversion for war, I should not like to have missed the memory of those first days…They did not know war, they had hardly given it a though. It had become legendary, and distance had made it seem romantic and heroic.
—Stefan Zweig (1881–1942)

Document 4

…I want you to know that if I am killed, I give my life gladly and willingly. .. [When I volunteered]. . . it was not from any enthusiasm for war in general, nor because I thought it would be a fine thing to kill a great many people or otherwise distinguish myself. On the contrary, I think that war is a very, very evil thing, and I believe that even in this case it might have been averted by a more skillful diplomacy. But now that it has been declared, I think…that one should feel oneself so much a member of the nation that one must unite one's fate as closely as possible with that of the whole…For what counts is always the readiness to make a sacrifice, not the object for which the sacrifice is made.
—Franz Blumenfeld, a soldier in a 1914 letter to his mother

Document 5

….the War in which we had refused to believe broke out, and it brought—disillusionment. Not only is it more bloody and more destructive than any war of other days, because of the enormously increased perfection of weapons of attack and defense; it is at least as cruel, as embittered, as implacable as any that has preceded it…It cuts all the common bonds between the contending peoples, and threatens to leave a legacy of embitterment that will make any renewal of those bonds impossible for a long time to come.
—Sigmund Freud, Institute of Psychoanalysis, London, 1915

GO ON TO THE NEXT PAGE

Document 6

Dulce et Decorum Est

Bent double, like old beggars under sacks,
Knock-kneed, coughing like hags, we cursed through sludge,
Till on the haunting flares we turned our backs
And towards our distant rest began to trudge.
Men marched asleep. Many had lost their boots
But limped on, blood-shod. All went lame; all blind;
Drunk with fatigue; deaf even to the hoots
Of tired, outstripped Five-Nines that dropped behind.
Gas! GAS! Quick, boys! —An ecstasy of fumbling,
Fitting the clumsy helmets just in time;
But someone still was yelling out and stumbling,
And flound'ring like a man in fire or lime...
Dim, through the misty panes and thick green light,
As under a green sea, I saw him drowning.
In all my dreams, before my helpless sight,
He plunges at me, guttering, choking, drowning.
If in some smothering dreams you too could pace
Behind the wagon that we flung him in,
And watch the white eyes writhing in his face,
His hanging face, like a devil's sick of sin;
If you could hear, at every jolt, the blood
Come gargling from the froth-corrupted lungs,
Obscene as cancer, bitter as the cud
Of vile, incurable sores on innocent tongues, —
My friend, you would not tell with such high zest
To children ardent for some desperate glory,
The old Lie: *Dulce et decorum est*
*Pro patria mori.**
—Wilfred Owen, British poet, 1893–1918
*It is right and proper to die for one's country

Document 7

His (the infantryman) role is simply to dig himself a hole in the ground and to keep hidden in it as tightly as possible. Continually under the fire of the opposing batteries, he is yet never allowed to get a glimpse of the enemy. Exposed to all the dangers of war, but none of its enthusiasms or splendid élan, he is condemned to sit like an animal in its burrow and hear the shells whistle over his head and take their little daily toll from his comrades…How different from the popular notion of the evening campfire, the songs and good cheer.
—Letter to the *New York Sun* from Alan Seeger, from the trenches in France, 1914

GO ON TO THE NEXT PAGE

Document 8

World War I Poster

GO ON TO THE NEXT PAGE ➔

Document 9

In the first place, I would like to observe that the older generation had certainly pretty well ruined this world before passing it on to us. They give us this Thing, knocked to pieces, leaky, red-hot, threatening to blow up; and then, they are surprised that we don't accept it with the same attitude of pretty, decorous enthusiasm with which they received it, way back in eighteen-ninety, nicely painted, smoothly running, practically foolproof. . . Life for them was bright and pleasant. Now my generation is disillusioned, and, I think, to a certain extent, brutalized, by the cataclysm which their complacent folly engendered. . . We have been forced to become realists overnight, instead of idealists, as was our birthright.

—John F. Carter, Jr., 1920

Document 10

The storm has died away, and still we are restless, uneasy, as if the storm were about to break. Almost all the affairs of men remain in a terrible uncertainty. We think of what has disappeared, we are almost destroyed by what has been destroyed; we do not know what will be born, and we fear the future, not without reason. We hope vaguely, we dread precisely; our fears are infinitely more precise than our hopes; we confess that the charm of life is behind us, abundance is behind us, but doubt and disorder are in us and with us…We are a very unfortunate generation whose lot has been to see the moment of our passage through life coincide with the arrival of great and terrifying events, the echo of which will resound through all our lives.

—Address by Paul Valery at University of Zurich, November 15, 1922

GO ON TO THE NEXT PAGE

AP EUROPEAN HISTORY FREE-RESPONSE QUESTIONS

Document 11

Countries	Total Mobilized	Killed & Died	Wounded	Prisoners & Missing	Total Casualties	Casualties % of Mobilized
Allied Powers						
Russia	12,000,000	1,700,000	4,950,000	2,500,000	9,150,000	76.3
France	8,410,000	1,357,800	4,266,000	537,000	6,160,800	76.3
British Empire	8,904,467	908,371	2,090,212	191,652	3,190,235	35.8
Italy	5,615,000	650,000	947,000	600,000	2,197,000	39.1
United States	4,355,000	126,000	234,300	4,500	364,800	8.2
Japan	800,000	300	907	3	1,210	0.2
Romania	750,000	335,706	120,000	80,000	535,706	71.4
Serbia	707,343	45,000	133,148	152,958	331,106	46.8
Belgium	267,000	13,716	44,686	34,659	93,061	34.9
Greece	230,000	5,000	21,000	1,000	17,000	11.7
Portugal	100,000	7,222	13,751	12,318	33,291	33.3
Montenegro	50,000	3,000	10,000	7,000	20,000	40.0
Total	**42,188,810**	**5,152,115**	**12,831,004**	**4,121,090**	**22,104,209**	**52.3**
Central Powers						
Germany	11,000,000	1,773,700	4,216,058	1,152,800	7,142,558	64.9
Austria-Hungary	7,800,000	1,200,000	3,620,000	2,200,000	7,020,000	90.0
Turkey	2,850,000	325,000	400,000	250,000	975,000	34.2
Bulgaria	1,200,000	87,500	152,390	27,029	266,919	22.2
Total	**22,850,000**	**3,386,200**	**8,388,448**	**3,629,829**	**15,404,477**	**67.4**
Grand Total	**65,038,810**	**8,538,315**	**21,219,452**	**7,750,919**	**37,508,686**	**57.6**

END OF PART A

GO ON TO THE NEXT PAGE

AP EUROPEAN HISTORY
SECTION II
Parts B & C

(Suggested planning and writing time—70 minutes)
Percent of Section II score—55

<u>Directions:</u> You are to answer the following questions. You should spend 5 minutes organizing or outlining each essay. Write an essay that:

- has a relevant thesis and supports that thesis with appropriate historical evidence.
- addresses all parts of the question.
- uses historical context to show change over time and/or continuities.

1. Discuss the major innovations and innovators associated with the Scientific Revolution and evaluate the ways in which these new ideas changed the traditional way of thinking in science, religion, and philosophy.

2. The Treaty of Versailles has frequently been described as the first step toward World War II. Evaluate the truth of this statement citing specific problems in the treaty that led to World War II.

END OF EXAMINATION

PRACTICE EXAM 2: ANSWERS & EXPLANATIONS

Answer Key for Practice Exam 2

Number	Answer	Right	Wrong	Number	Answer	Right	Wrong	Number	Answer	Right	Wrong
1	C	___	___	28	A	___	___	55	B	___	___
2	E	___	___	29	A	___	___	56	A	___	___
3	A	___	___	30	A	___	___	57	C	___	___
4	A	___	___	31	D	___	___	58	D	___	___
5	D	___	___	32	A	___	___	59	B	___	___
6	C	___	___	33	E	___	___	60	D	___	___
7	E	___	___	34	C	___	___	61	E	___	___
8	B	___	___	35	D	___	___	62	A	___	___
9	E	___	___	36	B	___	___	63	E	___	___
10	A	___	___	37	E	___	___	64	A	___	___
11	E	___	___	38	A	___	___	65	E	___	___
12	D	___	___	39	D	___	___	66	A	___	___
13	E	___	___	40	A	___	___	67	D	___	___
14	B	___	___	41	C	___	___	68	D	___	___
15	A	___	___	42	A	___	___	69	D	___	___
16	C	___	___	43	B	___	___	70	C	___	___
17	E	___	___	44	E	___	___	71	A	___	___
18	E	___	___	45	C	___	___	72	D	___	___
19	A	___	___	46	B	___	___	73	A	___	___
20	C	___	___	47	D	___	___	74	E	___	___
21	E	___	___	48	E	___	___	75	C	___	___
22	B	___	___	49	A	___	___	76	D	___	___
23	D	___	___	50	C	___	___	77	A	___	___
24	E	___	___	51	E	___	___	78	E	___	___
25	C	___	___	52	C	___	___	79	B	___	___
26	E	___	___	53	C	___	___	80	E	___	___
27	A	___	___	54	A	___	___				

HOW TO CALCULATE YOUR SCORE

Section I: Multiple Choice

$$[\underline{\hspace{3em}} - (\tfrac{1}{4} \times \underline{\hspace{3em}})] \times 1.125 = \underline{\hspace{3em}}$$

Number
Correct
(out of 80)　　　Number Wrong

Weighted
Section I Score
(Do not round.)

Section II: Free Response

Document-Based Essay　　$\underline{\hspace{3em}}$　$\times$　4.500　$=$　$\underline{\hspace{3em}}$

　　　　　　　　　　(out of 9)

Thematic Essay 1　　$\underline{\hspace{3em}}$　$\times$　2.750　$=$　$\underline{\hspace{3em}}$

　　　　　　　　　　(out of 9)

Thematic Essay 2　　$\underline{\hspace{3em}}$　$\times$　2.750　$=$　$\underline{\hspace{3em}}$

　　　　　　　　　　(out of 9)

Sum　$=$　$\underline{\hspace{3em}}$

Weighted
Section II Score
(Do not round.)

Composite Score

$\underline{\hspace{3em}}$　$+$　$\underline{\hspace{3em}}$　$=$　$\underline{\hspace{3em}}$

Weighted Section I
Score

Weighted Section II
Score

Composite Score
(Round to the nearest
whole number.)

Composite Score*	AP Grade	Interpretation
122–180	5	extremely well qualified
99–121	4	well qualified
66–98	3	qualified
45–65	2	possibly qualified
0–44	1	no recommendation

*Each year the Development Committee determines the formulas used to calculate the raw composite scores. The Chief Faculty Consultant determines how the composite scores fit into the 5-point AP scale.

1. **C**

Burckhardt's pro-Renaissance thesis asserts that the later Middle Ages witnessed a revolutionary "rebirth" of classical ideals, in which Europeans began to rebuild their world along a more enlightened, progressive axis, thereby shedding the repressive chains of the medieval era. Historians criticize this implication that the previous Middle Ages were "dark" and not contributive to the age of transition in the Renaissance. Critics claim that the Renaissance was not unique, but one of many periods of growth in European history.

2. **E**

The Hundred Years' War determined whether the kings of England were to retain vast land on the European continent and was precipitated by the claim of English king Edward III, grandson to France's Philip IV, to the French throne, subsequently occupied by the Valois house. Moreover, the English ownership of land in Guienne and Gascony theoretically established the English as vassals of the French king. English control of the Flanders woolen textile economy caused an economic contest, especially when the Flemish towns began to push for greater autonomy from France.

3. **A**

Henry Tudor (VII) ruled from 1485–1507 and restored peace and order after the War of the Roses, 1455–85. He successfully consolidated his Tudor dynasty, managing to conserve on imperial expenses so as to avoid dependence on taxation through Parliament. Through his employment of instruments such as the Star Chamber Courts, Henry built an empire of "Tudor Absolutism."

4. **A**

The Hundred Years' War was a protracted conflict with many causes and consequences, primary among which was England's ownership of lands in southwestern France, thereby making the English vassals of the French king.

5. **D**

Louis XI of Valois, the "Spider King," ruled from 1461–83 and was successful in suppressing the remains of the feudal autonomy in France through his governmental techniques and territorial acquisitions. He promoted the interests of the French middle class through measures such as introducing the silk industry and using middle-class councilors and ministers in his government.

6. **C**

Ferdinand and Isabella of Spain used the Inquisition as an instrument of royal absolutism as well as to enforce Catholic orthodoxy. In this program, many non-Catholics, such as the Jews and Moors, were expelled or forced to convert. Under their rule, aggressive movement into Italy won the Spanish control of Naples by 1503. They moved against decentralization and toward a strong, centralized absolute monarchy without directly abrogating the constitutions so as to avoid aggravating their subjects into revolution.

7. **E**

The Franciscans were a religious order established to work directly with the laity as an outreach of the Church, which was trying to combat its image of being wealthy and removed from the suffering of the everyday people. Nationalism certainly was a threat, as it endangered the universality of the Church. For example, the English opposed French popes, while the French protested the Italian popes.

8. **B**

Petrarch is known as the father of Renaissance humanism. Through his emotional admiration of the classics, such as Cicero and Homer, he called for a return to Italy's powerful, successful Roman roots. His writings helped the rapid diffusion of humanism in Italy during the fourteenth century.

9. **E**

The Flemish-Burgundian School of the Renaissance epoch was particularly attentive to the capturing of sentimentality related to faith as well as the extensive realism in its details of everyday life.

10. **A**

The plague decimated the local clergy in the fourteenth century, leading to an immediate opening in many church offices, many of which were then filled by uneducated, unqualified, corrupt individuals seeking power. This became a precondition of the religious reforms of the sixteenth century.

11. **E**

The German lands and people were technically governed by the Holy Roman Emperor, whose very existence was grounded in the Church. Germany in the sixteenth century was in a state of political fragmentation and economic depression. The princes of the empire welcomed any movement that increased their power at the expense of the Emperor's, thus fostering their support of the Reformation.

12. **D**

In the 1500s, the check on rulers' power posed by the Church was removed as monarchs obtained control over the Church in Protestant and Catholic countries. This led these realms toward absolute rule.

13. **E**

The Leipzig debates between Luther and Eck brought forth Luther's ideas that were contrary to traditional Church teachings and challenged the doctrines of papal infallibility and supreme authority. In this debate, Luther also proclaimed support for Jan Hus, who had been condemned by the pope as a heretic for his beliefs. Luther's 95 theses directly challenged the sale of indulgences, and his work also asserted that Christ's merits are shared with the individual believer through the believer's faith alone, not through external conduits, such as the Church.

14. B

Johannes Gutenberg invented the printing press, which printed with movable type, thereby making his city of Mainz the locus of printing for all of Western Europe. This invention caused a rapid diffusion of Renaissance ideas, feeding the desire for humanists to spread their teachings.

15. A

Zwingli and Luther differed in their conception of Communion. Zwingli saw the bread and wine as only symbolic representations of Christ's death, while Luther believed in the literal presence of Christ in the Eucharist.

16. C

Philip II's ardent Catholicism led him to answer the Pope's call for a renewed crusade against the Turks, which led Spanish crusaders to defeat the Turkish at Lepanto, off the coast of Greece, in 1571, thus ending Turkish control of the Mediterranean and considerably weakening them.

17. E

Industrial expansion did not occur until the nineteenth and twentieth centuries, which led to the neo-imperialistic motives of that later age of imperialism. Early colonization and exploration in the fifteenth and sixteenth century was primarily geared toward feeding the mercantile economies of the mother countries and for "god, gold, and glory."

18. E

The Thirty Years' War (1618–48) was instrumental in pushing western Europe toward the conception of the modern state system based on ethnic boundaries, in weakening German unity to the point of near failure in the Holy Roman Empire, in allowing western regions to develop economically, and in promoting religious pluralism, especially in the German provinces.

19. A

Henry was obsessed with the idea of Hapsburg aggression and strangulation of France. Henry clandestinely supported the Swiss and Dutch struggles against the German and Spanish Hapsburgs. While choice **D** is tempting, it is too narrow in scope. Henry was not only focused on strengthening the French control of the Franco-Spanish border, he was also keenly attentive to the Franco-German border.

20. C

Over the course of almost twenty years, Mazarin nearly perfected the practice of absolute rule, thereby laying the foundation for Louis XIV's rise to power as an absolute ruler.

21. E

Louis XIV increased the power of the central government through his creation of an effective bureaucracy. The Council controlled legal cases and could remand any case to its jurisdiction at any stage of its development.

22. B

The English conquered Gibraltar in 1704, only to lose it to the Spanish and regain it again in the Peace of Utrecht. The Spanish also ceded to the English Mediterranean land and the exclusive right to the African slave trade with the Spanish colonies.

23. D

James I's rule set the stage for the English Civil War, focusing on whether the king or Parliament had control over England. The largely Protestant Parliament was loath to support the marriage between Charles, James's son, and the Spanish *infanta*. This marriage was orchestrated by James, who was directly seeking to ally with the Spanish Catholic Hapsburgs.

24. E

John Locke (1623–1714) lived during the English Civil War between Parliament and the Crown. His writings propagated the ideas of a social contract–based government guaranteeing man with the inalienable right of property, thereby challenging James I's idea of absolute rule.

25. C

In his *Novum Organum*, Bacon (1561–1626) proposed the essential base of the scientific method, by which he reasoned that methodical investigation led to valid conclusions about knowledge. His ideas were influential in fueling the scientific progress of the seventeenth century.

26. E

This piece combines two symbolic elements seen throughout Baroque art in its depiction of Catholic tradition and its employment of chiaroscuro, the technique of using shadows and light to create striking contrasts that added emotional intensity to its overall effect.

27. A

These four Hohenzollerns, who ruled from 1640 until 1786, are credited with the rise of the Prussian state through unification efforts focused on strengthening the central government, the Prussian military, and the building of a mercantile economy, among other achievements, such as introducing a postal system.

28. A

Both Catherine II and Frederick II of Prussia ruled with decided absolutism, establishing a tradition of strong, centralized monarchial control of their vast territories. Catherine expanded and strengthened Romanov rule in Russia, while Frederick paved the way for the Hohenzollern dynasty's position of leadership in Europe.

29. A

Monet (1840–1926) was one of the foremost artists working in the Impressionist style, and his name has come to be nearly synonymous with the movement. Impressionist paintings sought to capture immediate sensory experiences rather than create pictorially accurate depictions. Impressionist painters worked in open-air settings using natural light, and they used quick, short brushstrokes to convey shifting sensations of light and color.

30.   **A**

The South Sea Company was a corporation of British investors buying ownership and exclusivity of trade in Spanish America. When their stock prices began to soar, many speculators demanded immediate payment in gold for their shares. In 1720, the South Sea Company could not meet these demands, causing the "bubble" to burst and other such economic crises to ripple through the British economy.

31.   **D**

France, Austria-Hungary, and Prussia all had major uprisings in 1848.

32.   **A**

Britain was one of the first European nations to outlaw the slave trade.

33.   **E**

All of these elements were strongly linked to European imperialist goals and plans.

34.   **C**

The British North American Act was passed in 1867 and was designed to allow Canada greater political freedom, while maintaining its alliance with Britain (which wanted access to Canada's vast natural resources). **A** and **B** deal with prior issues. Britain was very careful in dealing with the Quebec issue, therefore **D** is incorrect. **E** is incorrect because Britain, Canada, and the United States were generally on friendly terms by the middle of the nineteenth century.

35.   **D**

The Sepoy Rebellion began in 1857 and ended a year later. Victoria took the title of Empress of India in 1877.

36.   **B**

In *The Spirit of the Laws*, Montesquieu (1689–1755) sought to relate the different political developments of different regions to their respective climates and geography. For example, he asserted that despotism arose out of a climate that induced laziness, and therefore required the presence of an overbearing ruler.

37.   **E**

Russia lagged behind in the scramble for African lands, and instead focused on regions closer to home.

38.   **A**

The nineteenth-century British Liberal and Conservative Parties both supported home rule for Ireland. This provided them with a small amount of unity.

39.   **D**

The Romantics reveled in the power and beauty of the natural world while simultaneously celebrating the human spirit. Foreign lands, especially the Middle East, were frequently subjects as well.

40. **A**

Liberal forces in Britain demanded the House of Lords take a backseat to the House of Commons. The monarchy's power had been in gradual decline since 1215. The rise of the Labour Party and the continuing success of both Liberals and Conservatives meant that coalition governments became increasingly necessary.

41. **C**

Bismarck considered the Socialist movement and the Catholic Church to be negative forces in Prussia. *Kulturkampf* was his unsuccessful "struggle of culture" to end or limit their influence.

42. **A**

The Edict did very little to free the serfs, and their landlords retained the rights to sell land to peasants (or not). The reduction of services owed by serfs was at the discretion of the landowners. Serfs still had to pay taxes and were not permitted (nor likely had any means) to buy titles.

43. **B**

The People's Will (*Narodnaya Volya*) was responsible for the 1881 assassination of Alexander II. Reaction to the event actually led Alexander III to establish Russia's secret police.

44. **E**

Deism was a cornerstone of the eighteenth-century Enlightenment, wherein many intellectuals criticized the belief in supernaturalism and even denied divine revelation. Organized religion was considered a roadblock to intellectual achievement.

45. **C**

While it is true that Austria did not favor Italian unification (choice **E**), the quote is not germane to that policy. **D** is too extreme in scope.

46. **B**

Suffragists went on hunger strikes (they did not, however, encourage this in a prisonwide manner thus eliminating **E**), as well as set fires, and in one incident, a member of the WSPU committed suicide.

47. **D**

Compulsory conscription began in Germany, and most other European powers followed suit soon thereafter.

48. **E**

Britain had pledged to protect Belgium's neutrality.

49. **A**

While Wilson hoped the Fourteen Points would be the basis of the Treaty of Versailles, they were largely rejected. Many Germans felt tricked by the Points, but clearly that was not Wilson's intent, and the United States was generally not concerned about French interests at all. Also, the Fourteen Points called for colonial self-determination.

50. C

The 1939 invasion of Poland by German forces marked the beginning of World War II. The other answers deal with appeasement of Hitler's Germany, and preceded the war itself.

51. E

In June 1941, Hitler, against his generals' advice, ordered the attack on the USSR. While initially successful, it would ultimately be one of Hitler's largest mistakes. In December 1941, Japan attacked the United States, ending America's neutrality in World War II.

52. C

The Nuremberg Laws, which began to take effect in 1935, essentially took away the citizenship of Germany's Jewish population. Jews were not allowed to practice law or medicine freely and were forced out of Germany's public educational system.

53. C

The 1947 Marshall Plan was America's effort to stabilize Western Europe with democracy and capitalism. The USSR and Soviet-bloc nations were offered assistance but refused it.

54. A

Walter Ulbricht was a prominent Communist leader during the crucial early days of the German Democratic Republic (East Germany), making **A** the correct answer. **E** is tempting, as Ulbricht was a firm supporter of Stalin, who was determined to have East Germany as a satellite state of the U.S.S.R.; however, by the time Ulbricht was in power, Austria was an independent state, no longer under the direct influence of Germany.

55. B

The 1944 meeting established the World Bank and the International Monetary Fund. The United States was instrumental in the meeting.

56. A

The disastrous defeat at Dien Bien Phu shocked the French, who were ready to cede control of the area. The United States actually would take over France's efforts to stop communism in Vietnam. China was already aiding Ho Chi Minh's forces, and Stalin had died in 1953.

57. C

The Soviet blockade began in June 1948 and ended in May 1949. NATO was formed because this blockade proved there was a heightened need for a military alliance.

58. D

The United States actually opposed the ousting of the Egyptians and successfully pressured Britain to withdraw.

59. B

The success of the artificial satellite made western nations aware that Soviet technology might potentially be superior to their own. Soviet troops were sent to Hungary, but in 1956 Soviet troops were not sent to Cuba. The split between the Soviets and Tito occurred ten years earlier, and it wasn't until the early 1960s that the United States and the USSR met to discuss arms limits.

60. D

Each nation believed the other was distorting communist values. The Chinese especially favored active expansion. The USSR did assist China in the development of nuclear weapons (choice **A**). The Great Leap Forward was under way, but was not an obvious failure until later (choice **E**).

61. E

The storming of the Bastille on July 14, 1789, was fueled by anger generated over increased food prices and Necker's being fired. The Estates-General had taken the title Constituent Assembly and was not extremely radical (choice **D**). For the time Lafayette's forces remained loyal (choice **D**). Louis did send his guards to Paris, but not to reinforce the Bastille (choice **C**), which at the time housed no prisoners of importance.

62. A

The wrongful conviction of Captain Alfred Dreyfus, a French Jew accused of passing information to the German army, caused a political and ideological war between the convicting conservatives who forged evidence and the allied political left of radicals, republicans, and socialists. This conviction was later overturned.

63. E

Alexander II's call for heavy penalties against revolutionaries led to his eventual assassination by insurgents convinced that his autocratic reforms inadequately improved Russian society.

64. A

Both thinkers discredited the Enlightenment's primary commitment to reason as the means for discovering truth and explaining behavior. Nietzsche saw reason as suppressing individual creation and Freud saw it as only one of many determinants in human behavior.

65. E

Britain wanted to control Ottoman territories; consequently, it supported rebels in Ottoman lands during the war. The Allies wanted to remove Turkey from the war so as to weaken Russian supplies and end the deadlock on the Western front.

66. A

Lenin believed that labor unions inherently focused on immediate issues rather than systemic change within the economic structure. Lenin and his followers, the Bolsheviks, called for an urgent overthrow of economic and social institutions. These institutions were led by a small party of unelected socialist radicals who were more extreme in nature than the Mensheviks, who called for a more democratic and moderate revolution.

67. D

While it is true some atrocities occurred, particularly in Belgium, the British government went to great lengths to promote these stories, which were regularly reported in the American press. The Zimmerman telegram and the use of unrestricted submarine warfare outraged most Americans. There is no evidence that the British attempted to bribe American officials.

68. **D**

All major players assumed victory would quickly be theirs and internal political dissent was at first put on hold. Initial recruiting efforts in Britain were extremely successful (making **C** incorrect) and bids for American alliances (choice **E**) would come later in the war.

69. **D**

Kerensky's government did not survive long enough to establish a constitution. **C** is incorrect as Stalin was not involved in the political upheaval at that time. **E** is incorrect because Nicholas II abdicated to the provisional government.

70. **C**

The NEP (New Economic Policy) was a program introduced by Lenin in 1921, when many peasants were protesting communist policies. Stalin's economic programs were the 5-year plans, and production of consumer goods was never a Soviet priority. Trotsky was instrumental in military affairs, not economics.

71. **A**

Mussolini needed the support of the Catholic Church to 'help solidify his prestige and power in Italy. The Catholic Church did not overtly criticize Hitler or fascism and no pact was signed between Hitler and the Pope. The Lateran Pact was financially positive for the Vatican and no church lands were taken.

72. **D**

Most of those who died in the Putsch were Nazis or state police officers, not high-ranking Communists, so choice **C** is incorrect. Ludendorf was not killed; Hindenburg had no role in the plot. The Nazi Party was not banned. The attempted coup and subsequent trial did afford Hitler the venue to explain his radical views.

73. **A**

Chamberlain made his famous comments upon his return from his meeting with Hitler in Munich in 1938. The Kellogg-Briand Pact (1928) outlawed war. The Treaty of Locarno (1929) was an agreement signed by Belgium, France, and Germany regarding upholding boundaries. The Rome-Berlin Axis (1936) established the formal alliance between fascist powers Italy and Germany. The Ribbentrop-Molotov Agreement (1939) was the secret non-aggression pact between Nazi Germany and the USSR.

74. **E**

Hitler was bitterly opposed to both the Treaty of Versailles and the Weimar Republic. He consistently encouraged nationalism and promised to end the severe depression that plagued Germany. Statement II is incorrect because the Nazi Party emphasized that women should serve in the traditional role of wife and, more importantly, mother.

75. **C**

The German operation against Britain was code named Scallion. Poland's intellectuals were targeted, but not in the scope of Barbarossa, which was the 1941 drive into the USSR. The United States was neutral virtually in name only; the 1941 Lend-Lease program was an unofficial alliance with England that allowed the U.S. to supply the Allies with arms while maintaining their technical neutrality. Italy was struggling to maintain its limited African holdings at the time and was unable to launch an offensive against the Suez region.

76. D

The 1947 Truman Doctrine sought to stop any extension of communism. The communist victory in China and strong communist movements in the Caribbean came later. The communist takeover of Greece failed and the United States tacitly approved France's control of Indochina.

77. A

In a secret speech delivered to the party congress in 1956, Khruschev denounced Stalin's abuses. The speech, "On the Personality Cult and Its Consequences," was delivered in a closed session, and its text was not printed until 1989.

78. E

The Weimar constitution established primary guarantees of liberal concepts, such as universal suffrage and representative governance. Its flaw was that it allowed for the compromise of such rights under Article 48, which allowed the president to take nearly dictatorial charge in emergency situations. Nothing in the document called for the abolition of religious tolerance, which was to come later through the actions of Hitler and the Nazis.

79. B

The conflagration in the Reichstag allowed for Hitler to stoke fears of invading communists, thereby increasing support of his invocation of Article 48, which gave him near dictatorial powers in Germany and suspended many civil liberties. This allowed Hitler to target and eliminate many institutions that would challenge his power, including the press.

80. E

Picasso experienced the German bombing of the town Guernica, which was intended to create terror and demonstrate Germany's support of General Francisco Franco. Picasso's work was heavily influenced by the attack and presents a nightmarish depiction of the suffering felt by the victims amidst the horror.

SECTION II: FREE-RESPONSE EXPLANATIONS

Part A: Document-Based Question

Sample Essay

The young men that fought in WWI, most between the ages of 17-25, are called the Lost Generation for several reasons. With 57.6% casualties over the course of the war, over 35 million young men lost their lives [Document 11], leaving parents without children, women without husbands, and children without fathers. The place these young men would have occupied in society remained empty. They were, quite literally, lost. More broadly, however, the term refers to the profound sense of disillusionment and disenchantment with prewar society and its values that resulted from the experience of an unexpectedly long and brutal war. In the wake of the war, former soldiers often found it difficult to identify with or endorse the values and ideals of prewar society and drifted, searching for something to believe in.

One of the crucial factors that led to the outbreak of WWI in 1914 was that Europe was, in many ways, enthusiastic about the prospect of a war. The Franco-Prussian War (1870-1871) lingered in the popular imagination, especially on the continent, as a source of enmity between France and Germany. More significantly for the boys of 1914, it was also glorified, remembered in a romantic fashion. At the outbreak of WWI, as Stephan Zweig wrote, war "had become legendary, and distance had made it seem romantic and heroic." [Document 3] Moreover, as one contemporary recalls, "patriotic demonstrations had an intoxicating effect and excited warmongers to excess."

Many contemporary authors recall the popular support for a European war and when the outbreak of hostilities was declared, "there were parades in the street, flags, ribbons and music burst forth everywhere." [Document 3] Combatants on both sides were confident that they would be home by Christmas, covered in glory.

Politicians and recruiters did very little to disabuse would-be soldiers of their romantic notions. One recruiting poster depicts a winsome young woman in a naval uniform confidently proclaiming "Gee, I wish I were a man. I'd join the Navy." The same poster also plays up the opportunity military service provided for social and economic advancement, promising promotions for those who enlist quickly. [Document 8]

Young men rushed to enlist, seduced by "the thought of glorious adventure, and pride of being chosen to share it." [Document 1] Others like Franz Blumenfeld, a 1914 recruit, expressed no enthusiasm for the glory of war and were well aware of the possibility of death, but believed strongly in a patriotic commitment to the nation. Men like Blumenfeld were motivated by patriotic sentiment; the necessity to "unite one's fate as closely as possible with that of the whole." [Document 4]

Mere months later Sigmund Freud writes of a profound generational disillusionment, brought on by the reality of the war. [Document 5] In 1915, three long years before end of the war, he accurately predicts the "legacy of embitterment" that characterizes the Lost Generation.

Bitter disappointment was hardly surprising for the young men who found in the trenches a sink of horrors which bore no resemblance to the fields of glory that had captured their imaginations. One letter from the trenches describes an infantryman "exposed to all the dangers of war…He is condemned to sit like an animal in its burrow and hear the shells whistle over his head and take their daily toll from his comrades." The contrast with the "splendid élan" and "good cheer" [Document 7] they had expected—and indeed had been promised by elder statesmen and military leaders alike—could not be starker.

The men of 1914 not only felt shocked, horrified, frightened, and revolted by the war; they felt lied to. War poet Wilfred Owen, who was killed on the Western front seven days before the armistice in 1918, describes the full horror of the trenches in graphic detail and ends with an admonition to the men who were directing the war but not fighting it: "My friend, you would not tell with such high zest/To children ardent for some desperate glory,/ The Old Lie: Dulce et decorum est/ pro patria mori."

The Lost Generation, who had believed Owen's "Old Lie" implicitly in 1914, felt betrayed by the older generation and the Victorian values of chivalry and patriotism. These ideals were seen as empty and false and the Lost Generation adopted a far more cynical outlook on life and human nature. "Disillusioned and, I think, to a certain extent, brutalized by the cataclysm which their [the older generation's] complacent folly engendered," wrote John F. Carter Jr. in 1920 [Document 9], "We have been forced to become realists overnight, instead of idealists as was our birthright."

Physically decimated, disenchanted, and embittered, the generation that came of age during WWI was in many senses lost. Nevertheless they fumbled for direction. Though it is not represented in this group of documents, the years after WWI saw a great social revolution and cultural resurgence. The Lost Generation ushered in a creative explosion in arts, literature, and music through its rejection of traditional social mores and modes of expression. Throughout the interwar period, writers like Ernest Hemingway and F. Scott Fitzgerald changed the face of literature, while flappers danced to improvised jazz music throughout the music halls of Europe. Cubism, Futurism, and Expressionism flourished in the art world.

Though it is true that the Lost Generation was "almost destroyed by what has been destroyed" they continued to "hope vaguely." [Document 10] In the wake of the destruction the war wrought, the members of the Lost Generation were, in some sense, obliged to find themselves.

Part B: Free-Response Question 1

Sample Essay

The scientific advances of the late sixteenth and seventeenth centuries revolutionized most of what was accepted as the truth in medieval society. These advances influenced not only medical and scientific realms but also philosophic and religious modes of thought. Such discoveries inspired the creation of the enlightened ideas of the eighteenth century and built upon the foundation of modern European society.

Copernicus is thought to be the "father" of the Scientific Revolution, as he challenged the accepted Ptolemaic conception of the universe. According to Copernicus, earth was not the center of the cosmos: the sun was the center, and earth was merely one of the stars revolving around the sun. Copernicus refined Ptolemy's ideas into what was known as the heliocentric theory and consequently challenged the contemporary assumptions of many thinkers, such as Martin Luther, with his notion of the sun-centered universe.

The horizons of science expanded initially by Copernicus and his theories on earth as a planet were developed by many subsequent scientists, who espoused the same desire for exploration as their predecessors did. For example, Johannes Kepler expanded upon Copernican theory by establishing proof of elliptical orbits within a heliocentric universe, while Galileo Galilei first viewed the universe through the telescope and applied rational evidence to support further Copernican theories. Lastly, Isaac Newton in his 1687 Principia Mathematica *proved mathematically the existence of gravitational pull among the planets.*

In addition to astronomic discoveries, the Scientific Revolution revealed new knowledge about the human body. Paracelsus explored the world of germs and illness, theorizing that disease came from outside the body, while people such as Harvey conducted studies in the circulatory system, concluding that there was indeed only one, central system.

Such mechanical discoveries applying laws and empiricism to explain the world spread into philosophic and religious realms as well. From the notion that the physical world was determined through rational, predictable laws arose the notion that God was a watchmaker of sorts, placing the world into motion according to discernible laws and then setting it free to tick away and define the details within its mechanical self. Deism, as the theory was called, was grounded in an empirical conception of the world, the very essence of the Scientific Revolution.

Philosophically, such empirical theories produced derivatives in works by Francis Bacon, who rationally distilled a scientific method, and Rene Descartes, who advocated for reason-based, mathematically grounded conclusions. Furthermore, political philosophers Thomas Hobbes and John Locke both built upon the conception of the reasonable society founded in a social contract and a government existing for the protection of one's property.

In total, the Scientific Revolution inspired a newfound return to reason-based thought and empiricism, in aspects of scientific society and in areas tangential to science, such as religion, philosophy, and politics. Such ideas formatively influenced the philosophes of the Enlightenment, who built more upon the foundations of modern social and political thought. It was the coalescence of such work that led Western Europeans away from medieval practices toward a more rational, methodical investigation into the world around them.

Part C: Free-Response Question 2

Sample Essay

The 1919 Treaty of Versailles satisfied virtually no one. The Germans, believing that the generally benevolent Fourteen Points would be used in framing the treaty, were shocked and outraged at the harshness of the final treaty. The Weimar Republic—one byproduct of the treaty—saddled the Germans with blame. The Germans were especially angry at being blamed for causing the war and being forced to pay reparations. They lost some territory and their overseas colonies as well. France was allowed to occupy the Rhineland, and strict limits were placed on Germany's military. The Treaty of Versailles established a fertile soil for nationalist and extremist groups to grow in Germany.

The League of Nations, Woodrow Wilson's organization, was a major achievement of the Treaty of Versailles. However, the League proved to be an organization of limited power and influence, and when the United States declined to join, it had no way of enforcing its policies. Italy and Japan both felt slighted in treaty talks and were unhappy with the final draft. Both, of course, would be Axis Powers, not Allies, in the next war. With the Ottoman Empire and Austria-Hungary dissolved, literally dozens of ethnic groups began demanding (and frequently fighting) in Eastern Europe and the Middle East. Nationalist groups who supported the Allies expected to be given independence at the end of the war. They were generally disappointed and angry. Meanwhile, new national creations, such as Czechoslovakia, tried to form a lasting unified government in the face of economic and social difficulties.

Emotionally, World War I scarred its generation, and it left most of Europe's people with a great desire for peace at any cost. Many believed that so great was the horror of the war that never again would nations go to war. This attitude set the stage for the appeasement of Hitler in the 1930s.

It can be argued that the Treaty of Versailles, especially in light of the impotence of the League of Nations, did indeed set the stage for World War II.

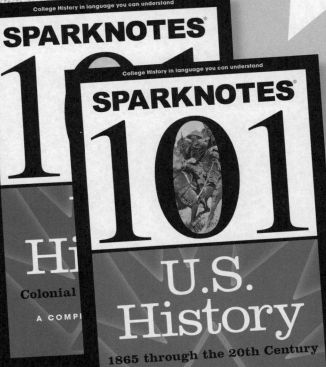